The AUSTRALIAN

J.O MANTEL

The Australian
Men of the World Series Book One

J.O MANTEL

This book is a work of fiction. Any references to real events, real people, and real places are used fictitiously. Other names, characters, places and incidents are products of the Author's imagination and any resemblance to persons, living or dead, actual events, organizations or places is entirely coincidental.

All rights are reserved. This book is intended for the purchaser of this book ONLY. No part of this book may be reproduced or transmitted in any form or by any means, graphic, electronic, or mechanical, including photocopying, recording, taping, or by any information storage retrieval system, without the express written permission of the Author. All songs, song titles and lyrics contained in this book are the property of the respective songwriters and copyright holders.

Disclaimer: The material in this book contains graphic language and sexual content and is intended for mature audiences, ages 18 and older.

ISBN: 9798482109267

Editing by The Picky Bitch Editing
Formatting by Mantelpiece Creations
Proofreading by Lisa @ More Than Words Proofreading Services
Cover design by Dana from Designs by Dana
Cover image Copyright 2020

Copyright © 2020 J.O MANTEL
All rights reserved.

For Danni and Lauren.

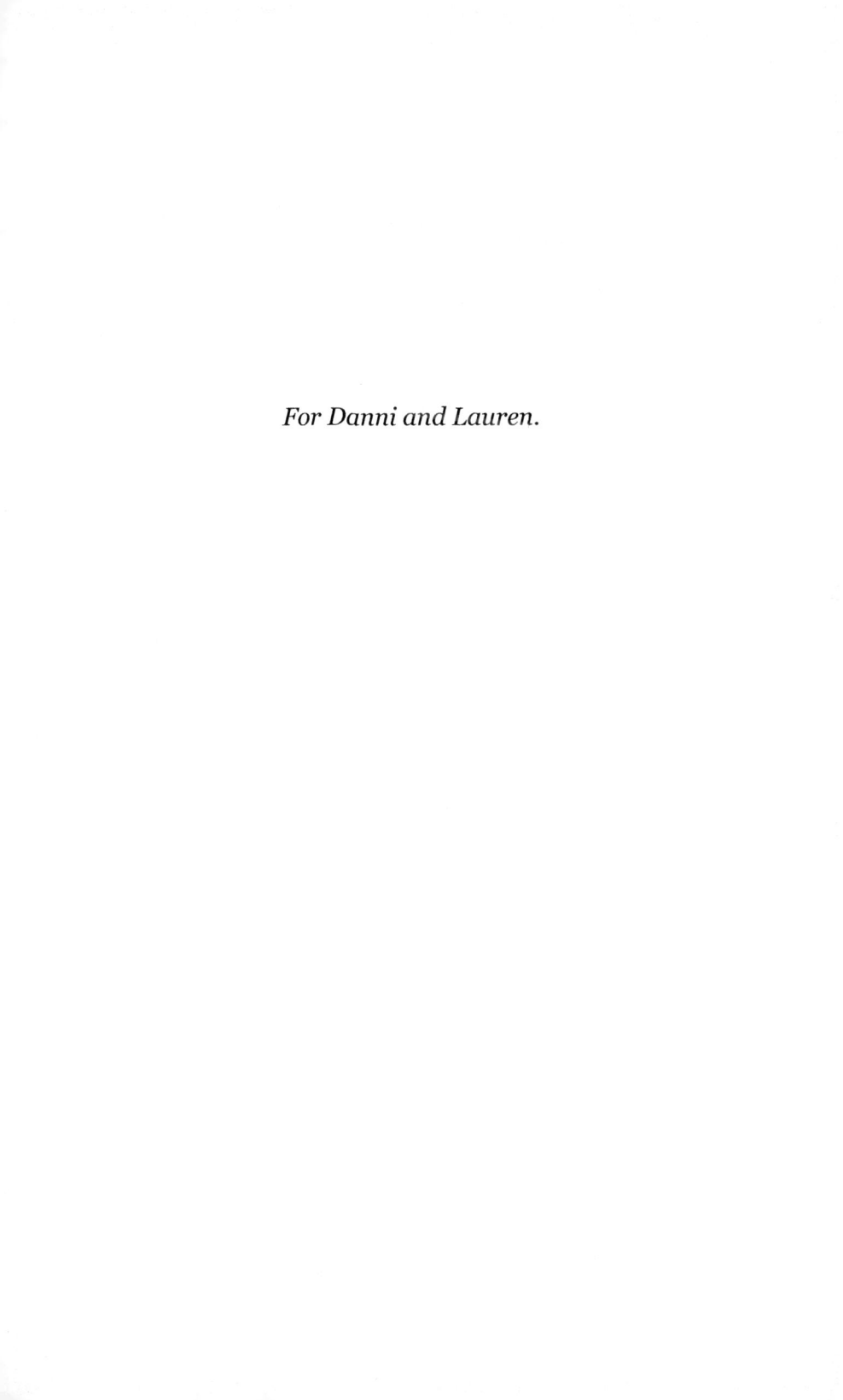

The Australian

J.O MANTEL

TAINTED LOVE
Prologue

You know when they say you've hit rock bottom? Yeah, well, that would be me. But it hasn't always been bad.

At the age of twenty-six, I was cast as the lead actor, playing a psychiatric profiler in a new prime-time serial, *Mind Crimes*. I'd had small gigs prior to getting my big break though, dating all the way back to the time I played Joseph in the Christmas play in elementary school. My parents were there, every year, sitting in the front row, cheering me on and laughing. Mom always said that one day I'd make a great actor. And she was right. Now, sixteen years later, after scoring the role, I'd won countless Emmys and Golden Globes, and owned my perfect Beverley Hills condo, thanks to my hefty salary. I had my dream car, an Aston Martin, and a hot-as-fuck boyfriend, Brodie. Did I mention I was also voted *People* magazine's Sexiest Man Alive? I guess you could say I had it all and was living life to the fullest at the top of the A-list.

I considered myself lucky that I was fortunate enough to have a job, one that I enjoyed and paid me well to accommodate my lifestyle. Mom and Dad don't work full time, and they've been the backbone to my career since I started acting. When I started making a regular income on the show, I wanted to make sure they were financially stable when they got too old, so I opened a trust fund in their name and deposited a large sum of money. There was also the house I bought in New York in case I wanted to spend long periods away with Brodie. I'm a philanthropist, so I've made large donations of both time and money to several organizations over the years. A fortunate side effect my popularity and reputation has been more exposure for these worthy causes. But my biggest investments over the years, have been in the stock markets. I've invested a lot of my money into the economy, knowing one day I'll get a great return that'll not only help me and my parents, but also my sister Kate and her family for many years.

And then ... it happened.

The Global Financial Crisis hit, and it hit with a vengeance, severely impacting the stock market. The Dow Jones bottomed out, businesses closed, and people were losing their jobs and turning to Social Security benefits. Interest rates went through the roof, and even those with excellent credit couldn't get a loan. Basically, shit got bad, it got *real* bad.

"Deacon?"

I raise my head from the script I was reading for the upcoming episode we'll be recording later today. My eyes meet with Lloyd's, the executive producer of the show, and I can tell he's nervous about something.

"Lloyd? Is everything all right?" I ask.

"Can I see you in my office, please?" he replies in a serious tone.

"Sure. Is there something wrong?"

"I think it's better if we discuss it in my office."

Before I have a chance to get another word in, he turns and leaves. I flip the page of the script and make my way out of the dressing room and toward Lloyd's office on the second floor of the CBS studios where we film the show. I push the button on the elevator and wait for it to arrive. I look around the studio floor at actors and crew hurrying in all directions, flustered looks on their faces. Some of them are even crying.

The elevator arrives and the doors ping as they open, so I step inside and press the number two for Lloyd's floor, staring at the doors as they close in front of me. As the elevator begins its short ascent, I wonder what on earth Lloyd would want to talk to me about.

Is it the ratings?

No. It can't be the ratings. For the last sixteen years, *Mind Crimes* has pulled in well over two million viewers weekly. The doors ping again, and I find myself on the familiar, dark floor where I've spent countless hours in production meetings with Lloyd and the crew. I head toward his office, and when I get there, his door is wide open.

I raise a hand but before I even get a chance to knock, he tells me, "Come in, Deacon."

I step into his tiny office and walk toward his desk.

"What's this all about, Lloyd?"

"Take a seat," he insists.

This must be serious; he hasn't even made eye contact with me since I stepped through the door.

He finally raises his head and stands, and I watch as he quickly heads toward the office door, closing it firmly before he returns to his desk and sits down.

"There's no easy way to say this, so I'll cut right to the chase. The executives sent word that the studio is pulling the plug on several low-performing shows, and we need to severely cut our budget to try and save our show from the same fate. Unfortunately, one of those cuts means that we need to end your contract … effective immediately."

I feel my heart literally skip a beat.

"Brenda is doing a major re-write as we speak. I'm sorry, Deacon, I'm afraid the episode we film tonight will be your last."

I say nothing at first, but then I cock my head and arch my brow. "Ha-ha, where's the camera, Lloyd, that's very funny."

"I wish this was a joke, Deacon."

I notice his sincere expression, "You're serious, aren't you?"

"I'm afraid so."

I feel an ache in my heart, and parts of my body go numb as I register what he's telling me. "No. No, this can't be. Surely things can't be that bad," I tell him, trying desperately not to lose my shit.

"I'm afraid they're worse than bad, Deacon. With the economy circling the drain, we're struggling to find money to keep the show going. We have to cut wherever we can, and unfortunately, one of those cuts is you."

Panic washes over me; this isn't happening, not now. Not when I finally have everything I've ever dreamed of. "What about the rest of the cast? Why am I the one getting the axe here?" I'm finding it extremely hard to contain the anger I feel building in the pit of my stomach. I clench my fists and place them on my thighs.

"Deacon, at 1.5 million dollars an episode, you're the highest paid actor. The studio can't pay you that sort of salary and still afford to stay on the air."

"But that's what we negotiated. That's what my contract states. It states that—"

"I know what your contract states, but it also states that we can terminate it at any time."

"What? Where?"

I slam my fists on my thighs. My blood is almost boiling, and I'm finding it more and more difficult to contain the sudden rage that's found its way through my veins. Lloyd stands and walks over to the filing cabinet resting adjacent to the window. He opens the drawer and flips through the files. He pulls out one of several manila folders and places it on the desk in front of me.

"Turn to page thirty-two," he orders.

Taking a deep breath, I do as he says and open the file.

"What am I looking for?" I ask with hostility.

He picks up his pencil and points to the bottom of the page where there's some tiny writing. I bring the paper closer to my face and squint as I read the small print.

Please note: this contract is subject to negotiation and can be terminated by either party at any time without notice.

What. The. Actual. Fuck?
"How did I miss this?"

"Deacon, you need to understand my hands are tied here. You think I want you to leave?"

"I don't know what the hell you want. I can't believe this. Sixteen years. Sixteen fucking years, and this is what you do to me. I thought you were my friend."

"I am your friend, but I'm also your boss, and I have bosses that *I* have to answer to. Look, don't you think if there were any other way out of this, I'd take it? You have no idea how much extra work this has created for us."

The one thing that really gets to me, is when people, or in this scenario, your *boss,* pretty much throws you under a bus and then tries to make out like they feel sorry for you, and all that psychological bullshit that goes with it. The thing is though, this is easy enough for Lloyd to say; he's not the one that's about to be jobless.

"What if I took a pay cut?" I blurt, not entirely convinced I'm even comfortable with the idea.

"You? A pay cut?" he asks.

"If it'll keep my job."

He shakes his head and pinches the bridge of his nose.

"Deacon, we negotiated your salary from half a million dollars, to 1.5 million over the course of the last sixteen years, as stipulated in your contract. Even if that were an option, I don't know how long we'd be able to go with it. This crisis has hit us hard. Everyone is struggling right now. You know, the news is saying that if the stock market continues to fall at this rate, this crisis could become worse than the crash that started the Great Depression."

Fucking hell.

"So, what? That's it, I'm fired?"

His silence is the only answer I need. I can't fucking believe this; my whole life, everything I've worked for up until this moment, is about to be taken away from me. I continue to sit in silence, my arms folded across my chest as I glance around the tiny office. There is a bookshelf behind Lloyd's desk, where all the Emmy and Golden Globe awards sit. Those he won personally are on the top shelf. On the second, third, fourth, and pretty much the rest of the bookshelf, are more Emmy and Golden Globe awards, one for every year the show has been on air, except for its first season.

"I'm really sorry. I wish there was some other way."

"How *exactly* do you plan on explaining my disappearance from the show to the entire world? I mean, Levi Beckett can't just disappear. I'm the star of the show, remember?"

He clasps his fingers together and places them on the table in front of him before raising his head and saying, "They're going to kill you off."

If there was ever a time when I felt like my throat had just been slashed, it was now. Was he fucking serious?

"What?" I say.

"It's the only plausible way we can get rid of your character to ensure he can never return."

"You're serious?"

He nods solemnly.

"You're seriously going to kill off Levi Beckett?"

"It's the only fitting way to have him leave the show."

"By killing him?" I snap.

"Deacon, I know you're angry. But you have to understand, this wasn't an easy decision for management to make. If they keep you on the show, it will chew so far into the budget that the studio will have no option but to cancel the show."

He continues rambling, but I stop listening somewhere after "*fitting way to have him leave the show.*"

When I successfully auditioned for the character of Levi Beckett, I remember Lloyd and our show producer saying that I had a gift; I was a ladies' man with the perfect ass, and the perfect body that all women would swoon over, and I'd be a ratings hit. Of course, I didn't tell them I was gay until our sixth season, after I'd won my fifth Emmy and Golden Globe.

Then there was one time shortly after, when I got caught with my pants down around my ankles and Brodie's cock, balls deep, down my throat in the green room. I was headline news for a couple of months after that. You should have seen the headlines: *Hollywood heartthrob Deacon Brady comes out as the first gay prime-time TV star.* It was great for my career at the time, not to mention what it did for the show's ratings each week. Now, here I am about to be fired and lose it all.

"I'm sorry, Deacon." Lloyd looks at me with sincerity.

"Yeah, me too," I reply, standing up and heading toward the door.

I head to the elevator, and after stepping inside, I wait for its descent back to my floor. I can't believe they're killing off Levi Beckett. I'm the star of the show—the guy who brings in millions of viewers each week—and this is what they do to me? Well, fuck them.

I sit on my chair, and in the reflection of the mirror, I notice Brenda come through the door. She walks over to me and throws the script on the desk.

"Tonight's episode, I'm sure Lloyd's already filled you in on your departure from the show?"

"He has," I reply, not making eye contact with her.

"Good. It's a movie-length episode, and taping starts at 5:00 p.m. sharp!"

She turns on her heel and storms out the door. Brenda has only been working on the show as the script writer for the past five years after the previous writer went on indefinite maternity leave. She has been a very difficult woman to work with. Always demanding and has everything set in her way. If you are out of line, she makes a point to remind you who is in charge of your lines in front of the entire cast and crew. Hell, she's got a bigger set of balls than I do. I have to admit though, she is the best script writer the show has ever had, and she *is* good at her job. She's sure given Levi plenty of award-winning scenes over the years. That probably explains why the producers have kept her for as long as they have.

"I just heard the news, I can't believe they're firing you." Tessa, better known as Bridgett, my on-screen wife of almost fifteen years, appears in the mirror.

"Well, believe it. Yeah, Lloyd called it budget cutting or some bullshit like that."

"It's terrible. I can't believe the amount of people that have been laid off today."

I swivel my chair to face her and raise my head. "There are others?" I ask.

She nods, a sad expression on her face. "Brandon, the show runner, he got laid off today. Cindy from catering, she was let go too. And just now, I heard Kyle telling Ruth that they're not renewing her contract. She walked out of the office in tears. I've never seen her so upset."

Ruth is another actor who I've spent a lot of time with on set, thanks to the producers writing her into the show as Jessica, the woman I've secretly been having an affair with for years. She's been an absolute delight to work with.

"Wow. I ... I had no idea things were this serious. I just thought Lloyd was firing me because they couldn't afford my salary. Things really are bad. Ruth was so much fun to work with, we got along really well on set. And Brandon, that guy was fucking hot, even if he is straight."

Tessa's lips curve into a smile as she places a hand on my shoulder and leans in closer. "I really am going to miss you. I've had a lot of fun playing your wife all these years, and for a gay guy, you really are great at faking it with a woman."

She winks at me, and I give her a warm and gentle smile. "Yeah. I'm going to miss you so much, and everyone else."

"Hey, this isn't goodbye. You have my number; we can always meet up for drinks. It's not like you'll never see me again."

"I know, but it's not the same as seeing you every day."

"You're a great guy, Deacon, and a fantastic actor. A guy with your profile can get an acting job anywhere once this crisis is over, and I have to admit, I'm kind of glad I'll be the one who gets to pull the trigger and kill the one and only Levi Beckett."

Wait, what?

"Excuse me?" I ask.

"You haven't heard? Bridgett finally finds out about her husband's affair with Jessica in the episode we're shooting. She catches the two of them in bed together after coming home early from a work Christmas party. She grabs the gun that she keeps hidden in her top drawer and points it at Jessica and pulls the trigger. She then turns the gun on Levi, making for the perfect exit."

I have to hand it to Brenda; she is a genius when it comes to plotting a great storyline; she definitely has a way with creativity and uniqueness. Killing off not only Levi Beckett, but also

Jessica Hamilton, is indeed the ultimate ending. But that has me wondering ... "So, wait, if Bridgett is the one who kills Jessica and Levi, then—"

"She calls the police and confesses to the murders, then spends the rest of her life in a jail cell."

"But that means you're out of the show."

She takes a step forward and sits her ass down on the counter. With her back to the mirror, she looks at me and smiles—it is the smile that somehow always reassures me that no matter what happens, everything is going to be okay. I guess you could say she melts my heart with that smile.

"About three months ago, I was approached by the producers of another show. They'd seen my work on *Mind Crimes* and told me that I should audition for an upcoming role. My contract was due to expire, and I wasn't entirely sure that I wanted to keep playing the ever so strong and powerful Mrs. Bridgett Beckett. So, I took a chance and auditioned for the part. The producers called last week and told me that I'd been cast as Brooke Forrester's sister in *The Bold and the Beautiful*. I've signed a ten-year contract."

She's leaving? After all these years of working together, one of only two women I've ever shared a bed with—even though we were acting—was leaving.

"You're leaving?"

She nods.

"But I thought you were happy?"

"I am happy, Deacon. But it's time to move on and try new things. I've loved every moment working here with you and everyone else, but there comes a time in an artist's life when we need to try some new art. You of all people should know that, right?"

She's right. I am very fortunate to have everything I have, and after countless awards and nominations, everything in my life seemed to be on fast forward. I'd played Levi Beckett for almost two decades, and I never saw myself doing anything else, at least not until now.

"I do. I know exactly how you feel. But … can you really see yourself as anyone else other than Bridgett Beckett? I mean, we were a team. LevBri to the world."

We both giggle, and I notice a tear trickle down her cheek, but I know it isn't a tear of sadness or sorrow—no, Tessa never lets that side of herself show in public. These are tears of joy and satisfaction. Deep down I know this woman is proud of the choices she's made, and I am proud of the woman she is; a talented actress, but most of all, my best friend.

"How did Lloyd take it?"

"Surprisingly well, actually. With the crisis going on, they weren't entirely sure how much longer they could keep me on the show. I was only guaranteed another twelve months, but I couldn't have that uncertainty, so I told Lloyd the truth. The producers at *Bold* have a much bigger budget, and the show has two more decades ahead of us. Their viewership is only one hundred thousand fewer than ours each week, so the ratings are there."

Even I remember watching *The Bold and the Beautiful* as a kid every night after high school. God, I was obsessed with Sean Kansan who played Deacon Sharpe. I always thought he was the inspiration for my mother naming me Deacon, until I later discovered he wasn't even in the show when I was born.

"Honestly, do you think the show will last without us?"

She gives me a look I know only too well, the look of certainty and determination. When Tessa has a hunch, she is usually right.

"Killing off one of the show's biggest stars? It's no secret that you're a fan favorite. Millions of women, and men for that matter, tune in to watch you every week. With you gone, honestly, I'm not even sure the show can continue."

"You know I'm really going to miss this, don't you?"

"Yeah, I do. But you need to look after yourself, Deacon. You need to venture out and try new things, meet other people. And as for you and Brodie, when the hell are you two going to settle down and get married? I need an excuse to dress up for a wedding, I'm Macedonian you know, and lots of cash makes for a great wedding gift."

"Ah, Brodie and I have *no* intention of getting married *or* having children for that matter. So, unless you know of someone else who's planning to get married, I suggest you find another reason to dress up."

She smiles and looks at the time. "We start taping in four hours, I guess I should head to my dressing room and learn my lines. See you on set for the last time, Levi."

She slides off the desk before leaning forward and kissing me on the cheek. "Looking forward to it, Bridgett." I laugh as she walks past me and out the door, leaving me with my thoughts, reflection, and let's not forget, a one-hundred-and-twenty-five-page script of lines to learn for the last time.

*T*hree months later …

The producers of *Mind Crimes* kept Levi's departure and my real-life exit from the show a complete secret from the tabloids, internet, and social media. The preview for the upcoming episode flashed the headline, *You will say goodbye to not one, but two of your favorites.* The producers had decided at the last minute to make that episode the season finale, making it the show's shortest season ever, and saw Bridgett, played spectacularly by Tessa, kill not only Jessica, but also her unfaithful husband, Levi. The performances earned the three of us Golden Globe and Emmy nominations, and also brought in the biggest viewership of over three million people, making *Mind Crimes* the most watched television show of that week.

I've watched the episode on loop over six times already. It really is bittersweet, and as sad as it may be, I couldn't be happier with the way Lloyd and the producers handled Levi's departure from the show. It's been just over three months since I recorded my final episode, and a week has passed since it aired on TV. People have been gathering on Twitter and Instagram saying things like *#CantBelieveTheyKilledLevi, #OMGNoMoreDeacon, #BringBackDeacon,* and that's when the realization hits me ... I am out of a job.

The past couple of months have been tough, really tough, actually. Every single studio has knocked me down, telling me they don't have the money to give me work right now, even with a popularity as large as mine. I mean seriously, there's only so many doors a guy can have slammed in his face before it kills his ego. I've spent the last few weekends with Mom and Dad, just so I can get my head around everything that's happened and not confine myself within these four walls every day.

The house has been too quiet without Brodie to keep me company.

It was near the end of my kitchen renovations, and not long after I came out, that I met Brodie online, and after months of cyberspace chatting, we finally met in person. Things kept going great after that, so we started making the five-hour flight between New York and California every other weekend. Though money wasn't an issue for me, the cost was difficult for Brodie ... so we concluded that if we really wanted to make things work, then one of us would have to move.

My phone rings, and I reach into my pocket and grab it, looking at the name displayed on the screen as I answer the call and bring the phone to my ear. "Hey, babe, you missing me already?"

The buzzer to my condo sounds, and I walk over toward the door.

"Hold on just a second, Brodie."

"Hello?"

"Mr. Brady, there's a courier outside for you, says it's urgent."

"Thank you, I'll be down shortly," I tell security.

"Brodie, I'll call you back," I say, and disconnect the call.

I open the door and head outside, where I pass security and meet the courier. He hands me an envelope, then prompts me to sign the tablet he's holding. I head back to my room, flip over the envelope, tear it open, and unfold the paper.

"What the fuck?" I say as I read through the contents of the letter.

The stock market has heavily crashed, Wall Street has been severely impacted, and all my investments have been liquidated.

I quickly walk to the study then open my laptop and sign in. I go to Google to check the daily news; the opening headline reads *Global Financial Crisis worse than the Crash of '29.* As I read through the articles, it becomes clear that America has been hit hard with the latest Wall Street crash, shutting down more businesses and affecting the global economy. The headline of the next article catches my attention: *Deacon Brady, the real reason he left Mind Crimes.* The article goes on to say I was fired from the show as part of production costs, but it didn't matter in the end because the show had been canceled permanently.

I go back to my online bank account, and when I reach the bottom of the page, my eyes widen as I notice my closing balance, $3500

What the fuck?

I scroll through the transactions again in case I've missed something, but the more I search, the more dismal my insides feel. Three-and-a-half thousand dollars. This can't be right.

There's got to be some sort of mistake. Where the hell did all my cash go?

I spend the rest of the morning going through documents and every single receipt I can find, but no matter how hard I look, the numbers just don't add up. My entire savings, everything I've worked so hard for, is gone, just like that. But how? Money was never a problem, and yeah, I lived a lavish lifestyle, but I never let a bill slip past me. Did I? How the hell did I manage to blow my entire savings in three short months? My attention is snapped back to my phone as it rings, so I stand and walk over to where it's resting on the adjacent table where I left it earlier. I look at the screen, and notice it's Brodie.

"Hey, sorry I forgot—"

"You got fired?" Brodie's voice booms through the phone.

"Brodie? Where are you?"

"You got fucking fired?" he says again, ignoring my question.

"Brodie, it wasn't my fault, the producers—"

"It's all over the god damn news, Deacon. You've made headlines all over the world. When were you planning on telling me?"

Wait. What? Why the hell is he so pissed?

"Tell you what, Brodie? The show finished over three months ago. You've been in New York. Why are you making such a big deal about this? Lloyd had to let me go, there wasn't enough money in the show's budget to keep me on. He had no choice."

I can hear his heavy breathing on the other end of the line. My gaze quickly flies around the room, and I feel my entire body fill with heat and anxiety. Brodie and I have had our fair share of arguments, but they never got physical. But this is the first time I've ever heard him raise his voice at me over the phone.

"So, what are you doing for work? How long until you get another job?"

"I don't know, Brodie. I've been looking. The final episode only aired last week. There's still enough attention in the media for me to get noticed. It's just going to take some time."

"Time? How much time, Deacon? I'm not going to work my ass off twenty-four-seven to support both of us. That was the only reason I—"

His words are cut short, and as they seep into my brain, the realization of what he's just admitted, hits me. I have to be certain, so I ask, "Wait … have you been using my money to pay for your partying?"

I hear him chuckle, as he replies, "I wouldn't say it was *your* money—"

"Have you been spending *my* money, Brodie?" I ask, the rage building inside me.

"I may have splurged a little, but what difference does it make? You're *the* Deacon Brady, *People* magazine's Sexiest Man Alive, Golden Globe and Emmy award winner. You'll find something else and make that money back in no time."

I quickly go back to the laptop and immediately check all my other accounts. As per the letter, everything I'd invested has been liquidated. I flip to a term deposit and pull up the page with all my transactions. As I scroll through, I notice several wired transfers to the Cayman Islands, and I suddenly make the connection.

What the fuck? Brodie's hacked the bank account and stolen my money?

"*That money* was all that was keeping me … us, afloat, not to mention, paying the bills and the renovations on this place. You had no right to use that money for your own benefit without consulting me."

"Since when have I ever needed permission to do what I want? You don't own me, Deacon."

What the actual fuck? Am I really hearing this? I can feel my insides churn, and my mind is spinning a million miles an hour. I swallow past the huge lump in my throat and ask the question that has been on my mind since this conversation started. "I'm going to ask you one question, and I want a straight answer, Brodie. Did you only agree to go out with me and be my boyfriend because of my fame and money?"

There is a moment of silence before he replies, "You can't possibly think there was *ever* anything between us, Deacon. I mean, we have completely different lifestyles. You're the actor. The successful one, the good looking one, the famous one. Everything was always about *you*. I was the one just tagging along, with my arm in yours, from one red carpet event to the other, pretending that we were the perfect couple. It's a hard life trying to keep up with *the* Deacon Brady, Mr. Popular and god's perfect gift to the men and women of the world. Of course, I wanted all that too, and the only way I knew I could have it, was with you."

That fucking motherfucker. He's been using me! After all these years, the son of a bitch has just been using my popularity and fortune, for his own financial gain.

"You fucking asshole! Because of you I have no money to pay my bills and the rest of the renovations on this house. I'm about to lose everything that I've ever worked for, and it's all because of you."

I take a deep breath and try to contain myself from losing my shit on the phone. The last thing I need right now is to let this low-life asshole think that he's won. No. I will *not* allow myself to do that. "I just want to know one thing, Brodie. Did you *ever* love me? Or was it just about sex and the money?"

I hear him chuckle, and it's all the confirmation I need.

"What do you think, Deacon?"

"You want to know what I think?" I clench my fist and grit my teeth as I continue, "I think ... you need to go and fuck yourself. When my lawyers get to you—"

"Lawyers? You can try and sue me all you like, Deacon. But what you have to realize is, you were the one who made the stupid mistake to purchase a home and put it in my name to avoid paying more tax. Which, by the way you can kiss goodbye, because you're never going to see this house again."

"Why? Why are you doing this?" I ask him.

"Oh, Deacon, it's nothing personal. Anyway, I really need to go. I have people waiting to see the man who stole Deacon Brady's heart from the rest of the world. We're done, I'm leaving. Goodbye, Deacon."

I hear the phone click as I pull it away from my ear and throw it across the room where it hits the wall on the other side, shattering to pieces. Our whole relationship has been based on a complete lie, and I was too in love and delusional to see it. For years Brodie has been taking me for a ride, parading around the streets of Los Angeles, with me on his arm, and it was all so he could be in the spotlight and take my money.

Within a week, Brodie has organized the movers to pack up his stuff and have it delivered to New York. Of course, he'd used whatever money of mine he had, leaving me penniless. With no income, my options were limited. Even selling everything I owned didn't give me enough money to make back everything I've lost. Through further investigations, I discovered that Brodie had neglected to pay his share of the bills, which had significantly impacted my credit rating and my ability to obtain financing. Things were starting to look really bleak.

"Ms. Mason will see you now, Mr. Brady," the receptionist calls from behind the counter of my lawyer's office.

Taylor has been my lawyer for years, and she was the one who negotiated my contract with Lloyd for *Mind Crimes,* and since the whole Brodie thing, and losing all my money, she's been taking care of everything. While her services come with a large price tag, she's been extremely accommodating of my situation, allowing me to pay her fees when I get my finances back in order … *if* I ever get them back in order.

"Thank you, Natalie."

I make my way through the closed hardwood doors and take a seat in the chair opposite Taylor's desk. The door in front of me opens, and Taylor walks through it. Her familiar long frame encased in a black knee-length skirt and gray silk blouse. Let's not forget the five-inch heels that complete her sophisticated, professional look that I've become so accustomed to over the years. Yep, as always, she's perfectly put together, fantastically fucking gorgeous, and if I didn't prefer a cock over a vagina, I'd no doubt have my dick inside her every opportunity I had. She wanders over to me and leans forward. "Good morning, Mr. Brady," she says, shaking my hand.

"Good morning, Ms. Mason, How are you?" I ask.

"I'm doing okay. Business is crazy at the moment, despite everything that's going on in the world. I would ask you how you're doing, but I think we both know the answer to that question."

I sit in silence and frown as she leans forward and puts on her black-framed glasses. She grabs a manila folder from one of her drawers and pulls out what I assume is my file, and places it in front of her.

"In light of everything that's going on, you will be pleased to know that I have *some* good news for you."

"Really?"

"Yes. But first, you've invested a large chunk of your money in the stock market, and unfortunately, with the crash on Wall Street, you've lost everything. Then of course, there's the house you purchased and put in Brodie's name. I'm sorry Deacon, but there's nothing we can do about that."

"Really, nothing?"

She searches through the file.

"No. The house is in his name, so legally that makes it his. If you try to sue him, he can take you to court, and if I'm being completely honest, he'll have a very strong case against you. Not to mention the excessive legal fees you'd have to pay. Is that really the path you want to take?"

I feel the tension I've been carrying since that damn notice arrived, ease from my body slightly, and I shift in my seat, giving Taylor my full attention.

"No, I guess not."

"You'll never have to deal with him again, though. Good riddance, as far as I'm concerned, the guy's a cu—"

"Ms. Mason!" I gasp.

"Well, he is. You're better off without him. Look, I think it's safe to say that this is the eleventh hour. You're broke, out of a job, and unless you come up with some money soon, you're going to have insurance brokers, creditors, and probably the IRS after you."

"So what do you suggest I do?"

"Honestly, your only option right now, is to try and sell everything of value that you have, including your house."

Sell my house? After everything I've worked for?

"There has to be some other way," I tell her.

"I'm sorry, Deacon."

Mom and Dad were always on my back about protecting my assets and fortune, so they suggested I get a lawyer to take care of all my legal and financial affairs. When I signed my second contract for *Mind Crimes,* we made sure Taylor went through the fine detail thoroughly, before making negotiations with Lloyd and the rest of the big wigs. Now that I think about it, maybe she had told me after all, about the clause that my contract could be terminated at any time. Perhaps I just forgot. Anyway, we told them that there were other networks who would pay top dollar to have me on their shows. In the end, when Lloyd realized what an opportunity he'd be missing, he quickly signed on the dotted line.

I sigh and lean back on the seat as Taylor removes her glasses, placing them on the desk in front of her. "Deacon, I've gone through your files piece by piece if there were any other option, I'd tell you."

Although I'd expected the grim fate, I guess a part of me was kind of hoping for a small miracle. Years of hard work, blood, sweat, and tears to buy my dream home, and in an instant, it was all gone, just like that.

"So what happens now?" I ask.

"We contact the brokers, find out what you owe, sell anything of high value, and then put your house on the market. In the meantime, I suggest you start looking for a new place to live."

My brain races a million miles an hour. Losing my home, and everything I'd worked so hard for, sends an ache through my entire body.

"Are you all right?" Taylor asks.

"Not really, but I will be. I guess it's true what they say, money can't buy you everything."

"This crisis has hit harder than anyone ever thought imaginable, Deacon. It didn't help that Brodie took all your money, but there are a lot of celebrities who are in the same position, if not worse, than you. Money can't solve everyone's problems."

"What about my Emmys and Golden Globe awards?"

"I don't see any reason why you need to give up those."

I swallow hard; my awards are the only memorabilia I have to show for what I've done, there is no way I am going to sell those.

"I have no intentions of selling them, they'll be the only things left to remind me of the life I have… had." She throws me a smile, and as she puts on her glasses, I watch her scribble some information on her paperwork.

After around thirty minutes, Taylor hands me the signed documents, I give her a kiss on the cheek and walk out of her office. Heading down in the elevator, I rest my head against the mirror and close my eyes. The only thing I can think about is Brodie and the life we once had. The life I thought was perfect, full of trust, loyalty, and love, and I wonder how it could all go so terribly wrong. The sex was amazing, at least I thought it was, since Brodie was never one to say much after we'd done the deed.

The elevator pings, and I step out into the foyer, walking through the double glass doors to find my car. As I sit in the driver's seat with my hands on the steering wheel, I take in the exquisite leather interior, knowing that within a few short weeks, I will lose it too. I buckle my seatbelt and head home.

Title: Tainted Love
Two - Deacon

      *U*nfortunately, even selling my home isn't enough. With the severe impact of the crash, I haven't made nearly what I paid for it or even spent on the renovations. With having to pay bills, brokers, and Taylor's legal fees, a chunk of the money is gone. I've decided that the best thing for me, is to give Mom and Dad the majority of the money I have left over. After losing everything I had invested for them, it's the only sensible and noble thing to do.

    By the New Year, on my final day in my condo, I've packed what's left of fifteen years of my life into three boxes, two large bags, and three backpacks, and couriered everything to New York where I've decided to return and live with my parents. As soon as they heard the news of my sacking and the stock market, they'd been calling me every day. I didn't want them to know I was struggling to find a job and survive; they've supported me emotionally throughout my entire career, but I didn't want to be financially dependent on them. Even though they knew the severity of the crisis, I didn't want them to think I couldn't do it on my own.

Fifteen Emmys and Golden Globes surround me as I sit in the center of the circle I've created with them. One by one I look at my awards as the last reminder of my career. They're all I've got left now.

Several hours later, I've wrapped each of the awards in newspaper. I place the key on the countertop, as instructed by the realtor, pick up the boxes, and make my way toward the door. Reaching for the doorknob, I pull the door open and take one last look around. With tears in my eyes, I walk through the door, and close it behind me.

It's only a few short hours later when I return to my parents' house. Thankfully, Taylor was able to make me keep my car when we sold most of my assets. Mom and Dad have been using my old bedroom as their theater room, and with nowhere to live, Mom is quick to empty my room so I can move back in. I'm thankful that their house had been paid for, using my first paycheck from *Mind Crimes*. I couldn't do anything less for them, which is why I made the decision to give them a chunk of the leftover money from the sale of the house. Their support of my career has been amazing, dating all the way back to elementary school. After Mom had two hip replacements, it made working harder for her. That coupled with Dad's part-time FedEX work, left them struggling to keep up the maintenance on the house.

My sister's husband used to help them as much as he could, but then they moved to Chicago with their twins—Sophie and Bianca. Kate's three years older than me and has her own life to live. They still come and visit every holiday—birthdays, Thanksgiving, and Christmas—but it's not the same as our parents having them around all the time. The economy will slowly repair itself, but times are still tough. I'm unable to get Social Security benefits, so I'm struggling with the limited money I have, and no matter how many times I try to give Mom money for my expenses, she refuses to accept it. I've auditioned for several new upcoming TV shows, but my huge popularity is my downfall, as producers want a fresh new face for their viewers every night.

"Any news on that TV gig you auditioned for last week?" Mom asks, placing a bowl of cereal in front of me.

"No. It seems that wherever I go, I get the same story. Apparently, I'm too popular for TV now."

"Honey, I know it's hard right now. You have to understand that the economy is only just starting to repair itself, and while you may have more fame and popularity than some, most studios just can't afford to pay for someone as popular as you."

While I know this is probably true, it doesn't help the sinking feeling I have in my stomach. I know she is my mom, and both she and Dad love having me around again, but I can't stay here forever. Sooner or later, I'm going to have to be on my own two feet again, without the help of my parents.

"I'd settle for anything right about now, Mom. I hate not knowing what tomorrow's going to bring, or having to worry about trying to survive, or if I'm going to have enough money to pay for my next meal. By the way, I got a call from Taylor the other day, she's managed to track down Brodie, and they're pressing charges."

"That is great news. He shouldn't be allowed to get away with what he's done to you. As for everything else, you don't have to worry about any of that, Deacon. You know your father and I love you and Kate too much to let either of you flounder.

If it hadn't been for you, we wouldn't have this house paid. Do you honestly think we would leave you on the streets with nothing? Even if you hadn't paid this house for us, you're our son, and we would do anything for you."

Mom sure has a way with words. With her hip replacements, it was very difficult for her to travel frequently to visit me. For years, she would help me rehearse my lines over the phone whenever Tessa wasn't around on set, All I need is just one successful audition, just one big break, and everything will be all right.

Mom places her coffee on the table, and she takes a seat beside me. "It's always the ones that we think we can trust that hurt you. We thought you and Brodie had everything, the new Hollywood 'IT' couple, and then he does this to my baby."

I see her eyes well up with tears, and I feel my own heart ache. Brodie was a part of my family for many years, and there was even a time when Mom and Dad were hinting at a wedding. I guess I can count my blessings that never happened, as I can only imagine how much worse off I'd be. I sit through the rest of breakfast with not much else to talk about. After helping Mom with the dishes, I head back to my room and stare out the window. I can't stay cooped up inside all the time, I need to head out and look for some sort of a job. I'm desperate, so I'll settle for anything right about now, because, as much as I love living here and being back home with Mom and Dad, I need my own space again.

I shrug into my brown leather jacket, wrap my thick, woolen scarf that my grandmother knitted for my thirtieth birthday, and slide into my Armani boots that were given to me as a present from the cast of *Mind Crimes* when we filmed our one-thousandth episode. I head out through the living room and notice Mom asleep on the couch. She gets tired a lot since the surgeries, so I try and make as little noise as possible. I don't want her to worry, so I write a note and leave it on the kitchen counter for when she wakes.

I open the front door, and the frigid air slams into my face. I put on my gloves and place my hands in my pockets as I walk along the sidewalk. As I stroll along the street, I notice young children playing with their parents in their front yards. The wind is blistering, but the sky is blue, and the sun is trying to poke its way through the clouds.

Walking down the street, I stop by several stores, and one by one I go inside and ask if they have any vacancies. Sadly, they all turn me down, telling me they can't afford to take on any new employees at the moment. Even Mr. Dawson at the tobacco store is closed today, and this is normally his busiest season. But it is obvious from the dimly lit interior, and the pile of unopened mail near the door, that he hasn't opened the store for quite some time.

I continue walking a little farther and when I turn the corner, I see the newsstand run by Mr. Anderson. I walk toward it, and one of the magazines on the rack catches my attention. The headline reads, *What Happened to Deacon Brady?* I grab the magazine and flick through the pages, just as Mr. Anderson pops his head out of the small window.

"Deacon, is that you?" he asks.

"Good morning, Mr. Anderson," I say with a warm smile.

"It is you. How are you?"

"As good as can be under the circumstances, I guess."

"Of course. I'm sorry, that was a poor choice of words."

"No, it's okay. I've gotten used to it by now. People see me on the streets but say nothing. It's like the world's forgotten all about me. I never thought I'd say this but, I kind of miss being approached in the street by a complete stranger and being asked for an autograph."

He reaches out a hand and places it on top of mine, which is resting on the counter, and gives me a smile. "Times are tough, Deacon. I'm sorry about what happened to you. But if it's any consolation, I think the producers handled your exit really well. It was a great way to finally say goodbye to Levi Beckett."

"You watched the show?" I ask, intrigued.

"Sure. I don't live under a rock, you know."

Okay, this is kind of weird. Mr. Anderson is probably old enough to be my grandfather. He's been running this place for over thirty years, since I was a kid going to elementary school down the road. I'd come by the newsstand every week, where I'd buy my copy of *Young Entertainment* magazine. I'd watched this guy get old over the years, and even in the chilly conditions, he was still here, with his long, grey coat, beanie, and fingerless gloves, making a living. I didn't think he'd be the type of guy to sit in front of the television and watch me, Deacon Brady, the young boy from school, act out erotic sex scenes on prime-time TV. Or maybe he was just really interested in the drama of it all.

"Excuse me?"

I hear a voice from behind me. I turn to see a man, around my height and if I had to guess, probably my age, standing there, staring at me.

"Can I help you?"

"Deacon Brady?"

"Who's asking?"

"I'm Dante Blaze." He holds out a hand ready for me to shake.

No. Fucking. Way. The *Dante Blaze?*

My eyes widen and I stare at the man in front of me as I contemplate shaking his outstretched hand. I reach for it and give him a firm handshake, and say, "I'm sorry, did you just say your name was—"

"Yup, I'm Dante Blaze," he confirms.

I release my grip on his hand and continue standing there, staring at the man. "As in, Dante Blaze, producer of *P.I.?*"

"In the flesh."

Holy, fucking, shit. This seriously can't be happening. I'm talking with Dante Blaze. *The* Dante Blaze, no less. This guy is an award-winning director and producer with more accolades than I can count on a single hand, actually make that two hands, and probably even both my feet. I'd seen him at the awards ceremonies many times, but I have never been this close to the guy. And now that I'm standing only a few inches away from him, I get to thoroughly take in the man. There is no doubt about it, this guy is absolutely fucking stunning. Mind you, I have absolutely no idea if the guy is even gay or straight. He always attends the awards on his own, and there is never any mention of a partner in his life.

Maybe he's just happy being single, or maybe he keeps his private life private.

"Wow. I'm sorry, it's just, I can't believe I'm actually here talking to you. I'm a huge fan of your work, I always dreamed of being on one of your shows one day."

He smiles, and his breath is visible in the cold air as he chuckles.

"It's an absolute honor to finally meet you."

I reach out my arm to shake his hand once more, and when he returns the gesture, I feel the firm grip on my hand, and our eyes stay locked the entire time.

"Mr. Brady, the honor is all mine. I've seen your work on *Mind Crimes*, you're a very talented actor."

I feel my cheeks blush. I'm used to getting compliments, but it isn't every day you get one from Dante Blaze.

"Thank you," is all I manage.

"I'd really like to sit down and talk to you. Can I buy you a coffee?"

Like I'm going to say no to this guy. I turn to face Mr. Anderson and bid him farewell, before turning my attention back to Dante. I stand beside him and we cross the street and head into one of the cafés. I give Dante my order, and he tells me to take a seat at one of the booths by the window. I walk over to the booth as instructed and remove my jacket, scarf, and gloves, before taking a seat by the window. Within a few short minutes, Dante walks over to the booth and sits on the seat opposite me.

"Okay, so I suppose you're wondering what all this is about?" he asks.

"More… intrigued, if I'm being completely honest," I say.

"I read about you in the papers, Deacon. I'm sorry about what happened to you."

"Thank you."

I shift in my seat, and I don't know why, but for some reason, having this conversation with Dante Blaze, makes me feel really nervous, not to mention embarrassed. It's enough that the entire world knows I'd officially lost practically everything, but when a TV producer reads about you hitting rock bottom, it kind of takes the cake.

The waitress from behind the counter approaches our booth and places a take-away cup of coffee in front of me, and another in front of Dante. With a beaming smile, she turns and heads back behind the counter. I bring the cup to my lips and take a sip of the coffee. Damn, it feels so fucking good to have that hot liquid ooze down my throat. I place the cup down and give Dante my attention.

"So, what can I do for you, Mr. Blaze?"

"It's more what I can do for *you*, Deacon. And Dante, please."

I swallow nervously before taking another sip of my deliciously hot coffee.

"As you know, I've worked on *P.I.* for some years now. Well, my time with the show came to an end about a year ago. Since then, I've spent quite a bit of time talking with producers from other shows, and after some extensive homework, we've come up with a brand-new concept for a show of our own."

"Concept, what kind of concept?" I ask, curiously.

"A reality show called *Tainted Love*."

"As in, Soft Cell, 'Tainted Love'?"

"Erm, not exactly."

I wait for him to continue, but when he says nothing and takes a sip of his coffee instead, I lose patience. "So, what did you have in mind?"

He leans back in his seat and clasps his hands together on the table in front of him, and for some reason, that maneuver just makes me nervous as all fuck.

"A reality show. Kind of like *The Bachelor,* only with a twist."

"What kind of a twist?"

He pushes forward and takes a sip of his coffee before focusing his gaze on me. "We want *you* to be our celebrity bachelor, who's looking for love."

Did he just say he wanted ME to be on his show?

"I'm sorry, what?"

"You're a very attractive man, Deacon. And you're exactly what we want on our show."

"So, wait a minute. You want me to spend the next three months in front of a camera, on some remote island, with a bunch of strange women, then at the end of it, I have to choose one to marry?"

"Not *exactly*."

Okay, this guy might be a high-profile producer and all, but right now, he isn't making any fucking sense. Whatever it is that he's trying to say, I wish he'd just get straight to the point.

He must notice the confused expression on my face because he chuckles and says, "Don't look so freaked out, Deacon. Like I said, we've put our own twist on this show."

"What kind of twist?"

"It won't be a bachelorette that you'll be looking for."

"Oh?" I reply, confused.

"No." He pauses before leaning farther across the table and lowers his voice. "It'll be a *bachelor* that you're trying to find."

Hold up, did he just say a bachelor? As in, a guy?

"You want me to search for a man?"

He nods in confirmation and smiles. Okay. Wow. Talk about a major plot twist.

"So, you're making it a gay bachelor-type show?"

"Metaphorically speaking. *The Bachelor* is a show about a man trying to find his true love, out of twelve beautiful, and single women. *Tainted Love* however, is an entirely new ball game."

I take another sip of my coffee and continue to stare at the man who has captured my attention in the short time we've been sitting at this table. He pulls out a rolled-up manila folder from the confines of his coat, and places it on the table in front of him before he continues. "Twelve men, twelve countries."

"What?"

"You will travel to twelve different countries across the globe and meet twelve completely different men over twelve months. You'll spend one month in each country with each man before moving on to the next, and so on. Our camera crew will follow you around and film your every move. Of course, when you go to bed, that's the *only* time the cameras stop rolling. And the prize ..." He leans forward conspiratorially, so I lean forward as well, without realizing what I'm doing. He whispers, "Twelve million dollars."

I think I physically stop breathing, and I can almost feel my eyes pop right out of their sockets. I stare at Dante, who's leaning back in his seat and casually sipping his coffee like he hadn't just dropped the biggest fucking bombshell of the decade.

"I'm sorry, did you just say twelve *million* dollars?"

He nods. "Yup, twelve million dollars. Enough money for you to make a fresh start and set yourself up again."

"But how do you have that kind of money when all the other studios are cutting budgets?" I ask him.

"This is my production company, so I'm paying all the expenses. I was smart enough to invest my profits wisely through my years on *P.I.*, and even with the crash of Wall Street, I've still got more than enough money to finance this show and pay you the prize money. You're Levi Beckett, every woman, and let's not forget almost every man, on the planet wants you in their bed, which means we'll get the views and ratings that we need every week to keep the show going."

"So, you're asking me to appear on this show for twelve months, meet twelve men, and after I pick one at the end, I win twelve million dollars?"

"Well … it's not quite *that* easy," he says.

"What do you mean?"

"Deacon. I'm offering you the deal of a lifetime that will no doubt, fix all your financial problems, and indeed give you a fresh, new start. But, this deal of a lifetime doesn't come without a price."

I swallow and feel my stomach churn. Up until this point, I was intrigued by what this guy had to offer, but now, I'm not so sure I want to know anymore, not if I'm going to have to sell my soul to the fucking devil or something.

"I'm not sure I'm following."

"Twelve countries, twelve men. You can do whatever you like in each country, whatever it takes to get to know your bachelor, but remember, the cameras are always rolling, except when you're asleep."

"But hang on a sec, I spend a month with each guy and then move on to the next? Talk about dump and leave them."

"Each bachelor is fully aware that you won't be making a decision at the end of each country, so you don't need to worry about any of that," he clarifies.

"Way to go making the world think I'm nothing but a traveling man whore."

"It's a contest, Deacon … a game even, something different. The world needs drama." "So, can I sleep with these men?" I ask, suddenly sounding very interested in his proposition.

"By all means. You can do *whatever* you want. But the one thing you *must not* do, or you risk losing not only the twelve million dollars, but also your heart, is you must not allow yourself to ever fall in love."

Three – Deacon

*T*welve million dollars!

Twelve. Fucking. Million! And all I have to do is *not* fall in love. After everything that happened with Brodie, I'm not planning on another relationship any time soon, so not falling in love is going to be a cake walk. After I agreed that I was more than confident of not falling in love, I had Taylor look carefully over the contract, including any fine print, and once we were both satisfied, I signed the contract with Dante. I had a week to pack before I would meet him at the airport where we would head to our first destination—Sydney, Australia.

Now that my week is over, I am going to be on a plane tomorrow morning. Dante and his crew are going to accompany me to each and every location. The promo clips for the show have already started circulating on the internet and television, but they keep my casting, and the plot twist of the show, completely under wraps for now. I was sworn to secrecy, and the only people I could tell were my immediate family. Needless to say, when I phoned Kate, she was on the first plane back to New York to give me a proper goodbye.

"You're really doing this?" she asks.

"Yeah, I am. I've given the opportunity a lot of thought. To some people, this may be a big risk, but where will it get me if I don't take chances in my career? This just might be the change I've been waiting for. You know? I'm grateful, not only for the financial side but excited to see where this leads me. How could I possibly say no?"

"You couldn't. You're my brother, Deacon, I know you better than anyone, even Mom sometimes. You never do things by halves. You're kind, loyal, and courteous, and you always think about others, especially with everything you've donated to charities. You're so career-driven and passionate, that's what I love about you the most."

Kate and I have a wonderful relationship; we've been close since we were kids. I'm her younger brother, and she's the smarter one, making all the right decisions and always mindful of other people's feelings, she always went out of her way to make sure I was happy and that I never gave up on my dreams.

"Thomas and the girls send their love and best wishes. They wanted to come, but the girls are busy with college and finals. They even said to tell you that we'll be watching the show every week, and you know how much Thomas hates reality TV."

My brother-in-law isn't a fan of television, unless it involves sports or finance. However, after he married my sister and learned that I was an actor on an award-winning show, his interest grew. Soon, *Mind Crimes* became regular viewing in their household. The girls were too young when they first started watching the show, so Kate recorded each episode and would watch them late at night when the girls were asleep. Once they were old enough though, they wanted to watch their uncle Deacon on television. Even at their high school graduation, all their friends and teachers wanted to meet the handsome Levi Beckett in the flesh and have their photo taken and snag an autograph. I love those girls, and when they were born, I was never away from them for more than a day at a time when I was on set filming. When they moved to Chicago, I traveled as often as I could so I wouldn't miss any milestones or school concerts.

Mom finishes cooking and sits at the dinner table with me, Kate, and Dad, who is leaving on a long-haul freight run to Canada tomorrow. Had I not been leaving for Australia in the morning, he would have started his journey tonight, instead he's decided to wait until tomorrow. This is the last time the four of us will see each other for some time, so he wanted to help give me a proper farewell.

"I know it's only been a short time, but it's been really great having you home again, son," Dad says.

"Thanks, Dad. It's been great being back, and hey, you'll still get to see me on your television set every week, it'll be like I never left."

Everyone around the table gives a forced smile, and Dad pops open the bottle of champagne that's sitting in the center of the table. We made it a rule never to drink alcohol at the table, but Dad has made an exception this time, considering I'm traveling to the other side of the world.

"So, Australia, hey?" he asks, pouring some champagne into my glass.

"Yeah. I'll be there for a month before we move to the next location."

"And where is the next location?" Kate asks.

"I have no idea. Dante wouldn't tell me. He said that I would find out the day before I leave. Apparently it's top secret, even to the other contestants on the show."

"You do realize that it's hot as fuck in Australia, right? They're in the middle of one of their hottest and driest summers right now."

I nod and twirl my fork in my bowl of Mom's homemade pasta and sauce, a dish that has been a favorite in our family for years.

"Oh, and let's not forget the huge-ass spiders they have," Kate continues.

"You two were terrified of spiders when you were kids," I hear Dad say.

"What do you mean *were*? The other day I found one in the closet. I swear, I screamed like a little girl, and Thomas came running into the bedroom to find out what the hell had happened. I told him that if he wanted sex that night, he had to kill the fucker before we went to bed."

"Kathryn Hope Sheila Brady-Sinclair, what have we told you about using that sort of language over the dinner table?"

Mom pins her with one of her all too familiar death stares. Hearing Kate being addressed by her full name makes me chuckle every time. We often wondered if Mom was under pressure from her family to name her and decided to settle on a bunch of soap opera actresses' names instead.

"What language? Sex? Come on, Mom, it's not like you and Dad are both prudes."

I can see my father itching to say something, but when Mom pins him with a look that says "Leave it" he refrains and goes back to eating his pasta.

"Do you know where you're staying?" Mom asks.

"No. I'll find out when I get there. I'm assuming we'll all stay in the same place."

"You'll probably need an interpreter while you're over there. Those Aussies talk funny. You know they call flip flops, thongs?"

"What?" Mom asks, raising her head and looking at Kate.

"Yup. I heard Chris Hemsworth mention it in an interview on *The Late Late Show with James Corden*."

"Now that is the most ridiculous thing I've ever heard." Dad snorts.

"I know, right?" Kate laughs.

The rest of dinner goes by without much more conversation. Mom, Dad, and Kate are all driving me to the airport in the morning, so we agree to call it a night early. I wander to my room and change into a pair of sweatpants and a long tee, then crawl into bed, pulling the covers over me, as I stare up at the pale ceiling. I cross my arms under my head, just as I hear a soft knock on my bedroom door.

"Deacon, are you awake?" Kate whispers from the other side of the door.

"Yeah," I whisper back, as the door creaks open.

The hallway light illuminates my dark room, as I see Kate's silhouette enter the room. She wanders toward me and sits down on the edge of the bed. I maneuver myself so that my back is resting against the headboard as I sit up, crossing my arms over my chest.

"Are Mom and Dad asleep?" I ask.

"Yeah. So, how are you *really* feeling?" she asks.

"I'm traveling to the other side of the planet to spend each month with complete strangers who I know nothing about, and the entire world is going to be watching me. I think it's fair to say that I'm freaking the fuck out a little."

"Understandable. Are you having any regrets?"

"No, not really. I've spent twenty years of my life in front of the camera, and millions of people have seen me shirtless. I was voted Sexiest Man Alive, remember?"

She cocks a brow and smiles. "Then why so nervous?"

"The idea of parading around with random strangers for twelve months to win twelve million dollars, I don't know, it kind of makes me sound like… how do I say this…?"

"A man whore?"

"Exactly."

"Are you serious? Deacon, it's not like you have to sleep with anyone to get the cash. Dante told you that. And besides, the cameras are turned off when you're in the bedroom, so the world would never know what was going on anyway."

I know in my heart she's right, and I've already resigned myself to the idea of never falling in love again, so I know that isn't going to be a problem either. I've watched these sorts of shows for years, and I've seen how they turn out. Everyone knows that the public end up feeling sorry for the loser. You know, the one who doesn't get picked, and it's the bachelor who's made to look like the asshole in these scenarios. Of course, I know it's all about the ratings—that's what the viewership is about after all—but did I *really* want that reputation after everything I'd been through? I can see the headlines now: *Bachelor Deacon Brady breaks yet another heart.*

"What's going on, Deacon? I can almost see the wheels turning inside your head."

"Nothing. Just thinking I guess."

"You said yourself that you needed a job, and this would no doubt help you make a brand-new start."

"I know, and it would. I don't know, I'm just being stupid. I'm sure I'll feel different once I'm there and actually filming."

"Absolutely."

I notice her lips curving into a smile. She's my sister, and Kate sure has a way with words, which is why she should have chosen a career as a journalist, rather than be a stay-at-home mom.

"Now, *you* need to get some sleep before your big-ass flight tomorrow morning, and so do I, if I have any chance of getting out of bed at the ass crack of dawn."

"I'm really going to miss you, you know that?"

"Der," she replies with a smile. She leans forward and wraps her arms around me in a tight hug. She pulls away and stands, heading toward the door.

"Goodnight." She gives me a smile.

"Goodnight," I reply with a smile of my own.

I watch as the door opens and closes behind her, and after a few short minutes, I can finally feel my eyes getting heavy. I slide beneath the sheets and pull the covers over my face and shut my eyes.

After being in this industry for as long as I have, you'd think I'd be used to early mornings by now. But even as I sit here in the back of Dad's SUV with Mom, and Kate sitting beside me, I yawn, despite being awake for almost three hours already. It is only a short drive to JFK International Airport from my parents' house, but Dad wasn't taking any chances for road closures and breakdowns, so he insisted we leave early and allow enough time to get to the airport. I'm shivering my fucking ass off, but the weather forecast predicts 116 degrees Fahrenheit when I land in Sydney.

"You know what's funny, I get to travel through time and into the future. At roughly this time tomorrow I'll be in Sydney and it'll be Wednesday."

"Yeah, that's kind of weird. You skip a day through travel and you're not even in a DeLorean going eighty-eight miles per hour," Mom says.

"And you don't have a crazy-eyed scientist warning you about the space time continuum and how even one tiny alteration can change your whole existence, either," Kate adds.

Yeah, I guess it's safe to say that my family and I spent a lot of time watching the *Back to the Future* movies during the long, winter nights when I was a kid growing up.

Dad takes the final turn to the airport, and I look out the window as we drive up the ramp and into the undercover parking lot. We grab my bags out of the trunk and the four of us head immediately toward the First Class international terminal. In every direction I look there are people: young children screaming, crying babies, and parents who look like they are about to die of sheer embarrassment. Yup, this is going to be a long day.

"Are you sure you've packed everything?" Mom asks.

"Yeah, I'm pretty sure."

"But you're going to twelve different countries, that's around four different seasons. The last thing you want is to get sick and they can't go ahead and film the show."

I raise my eyebrows at my mother and then frown. "It'll take more than a little cold to stop them from filming the show, Mom. Besides, I'll be on set most of the day, so the wardrobe department will take care of my outfits while the cameras are rolling."

"Passport?"

"In my hand," I tell her.

"Your visa?"

"Already taken care of."

"Vaccinations?"

"Mom!" I turn to look at her and say, "I've got it all under control. Stop worrying, seriously, I'm fine. You're acting like I'm never coming back or something."

"You're going to be gone a year, Deacon. That's a long time, for anyone. Anything could happen."

I love how my mom cares and worries about me and Kate so much, but sometimes, it gets quite annoying. Of course, neither of us ever told her that because we knew it would only make her more anxious. The line toward the counter continues to move at a slow pace, and I look at the time on one of the overhead screens, thankful Dad insisted on leaving as early as we did, allowing us to get through this congestion.

"Where did Dante say he was going to meet you?" Kate asks.

"In the First Class lounge."

Finally, we reach the counter. I place my bags on the conveyer belt and hand the girl behind the desk my passport and other necessary documents. After we finish at the check-in counter, I still have quite a bit of time before I'm due to board my flight, but I decide to proceed through security so I can just chill out in the lounge with a coffee. It also gives me the opportunity to get to know Dante a little better before the flight, seeing as we are going to be spending quite a bit of time together.

After biding a tearful farewell to both my parents, I then turn to Kate and wrap both my arms around her tiny frame.

"Make sure you check in on them from time to time, okay? You know how freaked out Mom is going to be knowing that I'm on the other side of the world and not under her roof, or within driving distance, where she can keep watch at any time," I whisper.

"I will," she replies, and I can hear a faint sob in her voice.

"I thought we agreed we weren't going to cry," I tell her, holding back my own tears.

"We did. I'm sorry, but this is going to be the longest that you and I have ever been separated. Not to mention how hard it's going to be on the girls not having their uncle around for the next twelve months."

"They'll still get to see me every week, just … not in real life."

"Exactly. It's not the same thing. I know we agreed that this was the best decision for you, and I am happy for you, really I am. But that doesn't mean that I'm not going to miss my little brother."

I feel her arms tighten, and I find it difficult to let go of her, but our embrace is interrupted by the loud ringing coming from inside my hoodie pocket. I pull myself away from Kate, taking my phone out as I look down to see Dante's name on the screen. I bring it to my ear. "Dante?"

"Deacon. Where are you? Are you here yet?"

"Yeah. I just finished check-in. I'm saying goodbye to my parents and sister, and then I'll head through security."

"Okay. I will meet you in the Qantas First Class lounge."

He hangs up, and with one final kiss and wave to my parents and Kate, I turn and head toward security.

As we board the aircraft via a separate gangway, the stewardess leads us toward the front of the plane and behind some curtains. I look around and notice a bar, and comfortable looking seats. Dante gestures for me to take the window seat pod, where I'll spend the next fifteen-odd hours on board the A380, Qantas flight to Sydney, Australia.

"Thank God for first class."

"You've never flown first class before?"

"Yes, but only for short flights, nothing like this though. I'm afraid of heights."

I know that sounds kind of odd, especially considering I've spent a lot of time flying over the years. But despite that, the thought of traveling at thirty-something thousand feet in the air, across the open ocean, scares the absolute fuck out of me.

I make myself comfortable in my seat and fasten my seat belt and notice the young stewardess who escorted us onto the plane only minutes earlier, walking over.

"What can I get for you, sir?" she asks Dante.

"Scotch on the rocks, please."

She smiles and hands us a menu each.

"Just relax, Deacon, you'll be fine."

We give the stewardess our order and she leaves toward the front of the plane.

He fastens his seat belt and grabs one of the magazines resting on the small table beside him. As I look around the aircraft, watching the passengers take their seats, it suddenly occurs to me that I haven't seen anyone else board the plane with Dante and me.

"Where's everyone else?" I ask, turning to face him.

"Everyone else?"

"Yeah. I didn't see anyone else board the plane with us."

He puts down the magazine he'd been reading and focuses his attention on me.

"You'll meet them all in Sydney."

"Huh?" I ask.

"The production crew are already in Sydney preparing the location for the shoot. After you signed the contract, we got to work immediately to finalize all the necessary details and permits. As you know, everything is shot in advance, and then edited as required before it goes to air around two to three months later. Basically, you would have traveled to at least four countries by the time the first episode airs. There will be times when the crew will travel with us, but at the moment, they're the ones who really get things started behind the scenes. You'll meet them just as soon as we touch down in Sydney."

It all makes perfect sense, Dante is a professional after all, and great at his job. He wouldn't have won all those awards if he wasn't. I barely know the guy, but I have complete faith and trust that he will make this work, for all of us. After all, his reputation is on the line.

"Sorry, I guess I'm just really anxious to get started, and to take off, so that I don't have to be on this plane any longer than I need to."

"Fair point, I'm sure it won't be much longer, we'll be on our way soon enough."

No sooner had the words left his mouth than the captain's voice carries through the cabin advising us that they were performing their final checks and we would be on our way shortly. I can hear the engines roar as my seat starts to vibrate slightly. The cabin crew performs the safety demonstrations before taking their seats. The plane slowly picks up speed as it travels along the runway, and within a few seconds we are up in the air flying above New York City and on our way to Australia.

Tainted Love

Four - Deacon

*A*fter an extremely long flight, we're finally here. Sydney, Australia!

Home of Palm Beach, the shooting location of *Home and Away* where the hot-as-fuck Chris Hemsworth, aka Thor, starred in his first ever acting role before moving to Hollywood. The weather predictions were accurate; the minute I stepped off the plane I was melting, so I removed my hoodie before Dante and I headed toward customs at Sydney's Kingsford Smith airport. There is a car waiting for us when we get out of the terminal, and in an instant, I'm swamped with flashes from every direction.

"Oh my god, it's Deacon Brady," one woman yells.

"Man, he's fucking hotter in real-life," I hear a male voice say from my right.

The driver steps out of the car, grabs our bags and places them in the trunk, as Dante quickly ushers me into the back seat. The paparazzi press their cameras against the window, trying to zoom in for a closer look.

"Deacon, this is Zac, he'll be our driver while we're here. Anywhere you need to go, or be picked up from, he's your guy."

"Hi," I say, staring at the man's reflection in the rearview mirror.

"G'day, mate," he replies in his Aussie accent.

"Kate's right, you guys do sound funny over here."

"Kate?"

"My sister back home. She told me about the weird things you guys say. You guys even drive on the wrong side of the road here."

"We say the same thing about you lot." Zac turns around and throws me a smile before turning back to face the road.

"Can you drop us at the Harbourview Hotel, please, Zac?"

"Sure thing."

"He sounds so funny, it's kind of weird hearing another accent when all I've ever known is American. What was it he said before, G … G'day or something?"

"It's short for good day," Zac interrupts from the front seat. "It's common slang here in Australia. You'll get used to hearing that a lot while you're here, especially when you're recognized on the streets."

I'm used to random strangers approaching me in the streets and asking me for a selfie or an autograph while I was working on television. I never really did much traveling, except of course when I visited Brodie, and I'd never been out of America. It's kind of freaking me out a little, knowing that people in another country would actually be stopping me on the street to ask for my autograph.

"Are you a fan of *Mind Crimes*?" I ask Zac, not really sure why, or what sort of reaction I'm expecting from the guy; I mean, we'd only just met.

"My wife is. She used to watch you every single week. I'm pretty sure you were the background picture on her phone for a long time. I think she may even have a few posters of you, hidden somewhere in the bedroom."

I'm used to women plastering me all over merchandise, hell, I've even had women throw their bras at me to sign, and one woman even wanted me to sign one of her breasts at the Emmys last year.

"Yeah, I hear that a lot," I say.

I look out my window and notice the hazy blue sky with the evident smell of smoke in the air.

"It's so hazy," I say.

"It's from all the bushfires currently burning in our state."

I look up and notice Zac's eyes in the rearview mirror as he watches the road ahead of him. "Australia is going through its worst ever bushfire season, they're calling this the 'Black Summer.' Almost every single state in the country is on fire right now. Some parts of Australia have the worst air quality in the world at the moment; it's toxic and hazardous for everyone. Sydney is such a beautiful city, and for months now it's been darkened by this thick, smokey haze."

I'd seen the news about the fires happening here, but I had no idea the full extent of the disaster. Being here now, and seeing all the haze around this beautiful city, takes me back to the days when I saw the news of New York City blackened for weeks after September 11. Dante reassures me as I press my head to the window to look up at the sky. "The fires are still burning, but I've been assured by the local councils that it's safe for us to shoot where we are. However, as soon as we get the notification of any danger, shooting will cease until further notice and we'll evacuate. Okay?"

I nod as Zac takes a left turn, and as I look out my window again, I notice the familiar famous arched architectural wonder that I've only ever seen in magazines, online or on the television. The Sydney Harbour Bridge. As we drive in the center lane, I look over at Dante, who's looking out the open window, no doubt admiring the almost fifty-three-thousand tons of steel that was used to construct the bridge. After Dante told me I would be traveling to Australia for his show, I quickly researched everything I needed to know about the famous city Down Under.

"You know, we won't be filming on weekends." Dante pulls his head back inside the car and continues, "That gives us enough time to climb this thing."

Did he say *climb*?

"Sorry, what?" I ask, looking at him, horrified.

"The bridge climb. I don't know a lot about it, but apparently you strap yourself to a harness with a group of other people, and you climb this bridge. There's steel railing, an expert, and you're equipped with safety gear. Sounds pretty cool, right?"

Cool is *not* how it sounds at all.

"You want to know how it sounds?" I ask, pinning him with a death stare. "It sounds like you're out of your ever-loving mind. I told you how I feel about heights," I remind him.

He says nothing but raises his brow at me and picks up his phone, probably checking his messages. We continue driving across the bridge before Zac takes a left turn down a steep road, and after going a little farther, we stop outside a building with the words Harbourview Hotel written across the front entrance.

"I'll grab the bags from the boot," Zac says, getting out of the driver's seat and making his way to the back of the car.

"Did he just say he was getting the bags out of a boot?"

"They call a trunk a boot here."

I burst out laughing, as I say, "Now that is the stupidest thing I've ever heard."

Grabbing our bags, Zac heads inside the hotel and proceeds to the concierge counter. Dante walks ahead of me and joins Zac at the counter. I reach into my pocket and pull out my phone. Looking at the time, I notice it's after five in the afternoon, which means it's early in New York. Deciding not to call my parents and freak them out, I text Kate instead, knowing she'll check the message when she wakes in the morning. To my surprise however, her response is almost instant.

KATE: Glad to hear you've arrived safe. I'd worked out the approximate time you would land, so I decided to wait up until I heard from you. How's Australia?

I should have known better than to assume Kate would be asleep before hearing from me. When we were teens, it was usually me who stayed awake and waited for her when she got home late from her dates. My, how the years have flown by and times have changed. With a smile, I send my reply.

I haven't really seen much. Just arrived at the hotel. Came straight from the airport. And what would you have done if I *didn't* text?

KATE: I would have activated the secret GPS tracking device I installed on your phone. LOL.

My sister sure has a sense of humor. The sad reality is though, I know she's not kidding.

Go to sleep. I'm just at check-in before I head to my room. I'll call or text you tomorrow. Give my love to the girls, and let Mom and Dad know I'm okay.

KATE: Okay. Goodnight.

Dante and Zac finish with the receptionist and walk toward me. I lean against one of the pillars and fold my arms across my chest as I yawn.

"Tired?" Dante asks.

"Exhausted. Must be the jet lag starting to kick in."

"Well, best we get to our rooms so we can get some sleep."

He hands me my bags and grabs his own before telling Zac to move the car and that we'll contact him in the morning when we're ready for him. We head toward the elevator, and when the doors open, we step inside. I move to the back of the elevator and rest my back against the mirrored wall. I look at Dante as he presses the number four on the keypad. The doors close and the elevator starts to make its ascent.

"Weren't we supposed to be meeting the others?" I ask, recalling our conversation on the plane prior to leaving home, about meeting the production crew.

"They're meeting us for breakfast tomorrow morning, down at the restaurant," he says as the elevator comes to a stop on our floor.

The doors open and we step out into the carpeted corridor, a row of paintings lining the wall. I look out the window on my left and catch a better view of the Sydney Harbour Bridge. Beneath it, I see a modern expressionist structure, with windows that look like shells or spheres, and it's then I recognize the building as the Sydney Opera House. Turning back, I notice too late someone walking past me in the opposite direction and crash into them.

"Oh, excuse me," I say, as I look at the man I walked into.

"That's okay," he replies in his Australian accent.

We stand there for a few seconds, and I can't help but notice his gorgeous dark brown eyes and sweet baby face.

"I'm so sorry. I should have been watching where I was going."

"No harm done." He smiles.

He looks at me a little longer and squints his eyes. "You look very familiar. Do I know you from somewhere?"

I return a smile of my own, and my eyes wander up and down his body. Something about this guy screams sophistication. He is a little shorter than me, and definitely has to be in his early twenties, if I was guessing. He's wearing shorts, flip flops, and a black tee, and the guy is deliciously attractive.

I stretch out my hand and begin to say, "Hi, I'm—"

"Deacon, this is your room," I hear Dante's voice interrupt from up ahead where he's stopped outside one of the rooms.

I turn back to look at the man, who is now walking down the corridor toward the elevator we'd just vacated. I watch as he vanishes out of sight through the elevator doors, and I hear Dante call my name again.

"Yeah, coming," I reply, and make my way toward the room.

TITLE *Tainted Love*

DIRECTOR Five - Deacon

CAMERA

DATE | **SCENE** | **TAKE**

It's after 10:00 a.m. the following morning when Dante knocks on the door to my room. He tells me the production crew for *Tainted Love* is downstairs in the restaurant waiting for us, so I quickly get out of bed and shower. I'd actually had a pleasant night's sleep, which hadn't happened since I'd been fired from *Mind Crimes,* but the jet lag had kicked my ass, and I'd slept like a baby.

I lift my suitcase onto the bed and sort through the limited clothing I'd packed. Dante told me to pack light as I'd be wearing clothing from their wardrobe department on the days we'd be filming. I check the weather app on my phone; Sydney was forecast to reach a high of 48 degrees Celsius, which was around 118 Fahrenheit. In other words, it was going to be hot as fuck outside, so I take out my shorts and a white tee. I head to the bathroom and quickly splash on some cologne and style my hair, before heading out.

When I get to the restaurant Dante told me to meet them at, I notice him sitting at one of the tables by the window with a group of people. I wander toward them and take my seat next to Dante.

"And this is Deacon," Dante says with a smile.

One by one he introduces me to the entire production crew who we'll be working with. Dante goes through the intense filming schedule, which will involve ten to twelve hours of shooting each day, Monday through Friday. My weekend schedule is clear, which means I have time to see the many wonders of Sydney. But there is one thing they still haven't told me: when I'll be introduced to the bachelors.

"So, when do I get to meet the contestants?" I ask.

"I was wondering when you'd ask that question," Dante says.

He stands up and wanders over to a door behind the counter and disappears. A few minutes later, he emerges from behind the same door, and there is a guy walking beside him who looks extremely familiar. As they approach the table, I get a closer look at the guy and realize he is the same man I'd run into last night when I was heading for my room.

"Steve. I'd like you to meet—"

I stand up and hold out my hand, essentially cutting Dante off. "Deacon," I introduce myself. He tilts his head and eyes me speculatively.

"As in Deacon Brady, from the show *Mind Crimes*?"

"The one and only."

"I thought you looked familiar when I ran into you last night. I'm a huge fan of the show, you're a great actor."

"Thank you," I say, and I feel him squeeze my hand as he shakes it.

Steve takes the seat beside Dante, and I wait a few moments for the rest of the contestants to walk through the door, but no one comes.

"When do I meet the rest of the contestants?" I ask, looking at Dante.

"Funny you should ask that, Deacon. There *are* no other contestants."

"I'm sorry?" I question, confused by his answer.

"I wanted to wait until we were in Australia, and you'd met the rest of the production crew before I revealed the twist of the show."

"Twist? Another twist? You already told me it was going to be a dude and not a woman I'd be searching for."

"Correct. But what I *didn't* tell you, was that we'd already short-listed our bachelor. You see, we wanted our show to be different from all the other reality, love story shows out there. So when the producers and I came up with the idea for it, we decided that we'd be the ones to pick the bachelor for you, from each country, and then *you'd* spend the entire month with each man. By the end of the twelve months, you would then make your choice which of the twelve men you had the best connection with, or who you declared your bachelor. After that, you would be awarded your twelve million dollars, provided you didn't break the rule, and your bachelor would receive their consolation prize."

I'm not entirely sure I've heard him correctly, so I ask, "So let me get this straight, you're telling me that there are no other contestants? It's just me and Steve?"

"That's correct. It'll be the same in each country, your bachelor will already be chosen for you when you arrive."

"Well, that kind of puts a new twist on things," I say.

"That's the point. *Tainted Love* will be different to anything we've seen on TV before."

I wasn't really into reality shows, and when Dante approached me to be a part of his new show, I quickly jumped on the opportunity, knowing this could potentially kick-start my career towards another direction.

According to him, I'm going to be the star of this show, but what's in it for him?

"Dante?"

"Yes, Deacon?"

"Can … can I speak to you in private for a sec, please?"

I stand from my seat and head toward the bathroom door. A few minutes later I hear the door open and close again. I look in the mirror and see Dante standing behind me.

"Odd place to have a conversation," he says.

I spin around so that I'm facing him, and say, "Dante, I have to know, what's in it for you?"

"I'm not sure I know what you mean?"

"This. The show. What's in it for you when all this is over?"

"Are you suggesting there's some hidden agenda behind all this?"

I say nothing for a moment and try to choose my words carefully. The last thing I want is to piss off this guy and have him pull the pin on the entire project.

"Why did you pick me? Out of all the celebrities you could have chosen, why did you come to me?"

"Because I saw what everyone else is going to see."

"And what's that?" I ask.

"Sex appeal."

Wait, did he just say, *sex appeal*?

"You're a great looking guy, Deacon. You're everything the men and women want, not to mention you'll blow our ratings through the roof. I've already said all this to you, why the insecurity?"

I turn to face the mirror once more, and my eyes meet with his as I say, "I was Levi Beckett for sixteen years. Lloyd told me that everyone loved him, and he was the reason the show lasted as long as it did. If that were true, then why was I fired?"

"The same reason the show was canceled, because of production costs due to the global financial crisis."

"Exactly. How…?" I pause and hold back the lump that has been sitting in my throat since we arrived at the restaurant this morning.

"You're worried the same thing is going to happen with my show, aren't you?"

"I'm sorry, but you have to understand where I'm coming from in all of this. If the ratings flop and the show is canceled, you still have enough money to live a comfortable life, and the reputation of a great director. But me, I not only lose my job, again, but I'm left penniless."

He considers me for a moment and takes a step forward, placing a hand on my shoulder as he spins me around to face him.

"Do you think I'd have taken a chance with you if I didn't think this would work? Like all new things, there are risks, Deacon. But I can assure you, the networks agree with us that including a twist will have the viewers riveted and waiting for the next episode; it'll be a positive game-changer."

My insecurity is screaming for me to tell this guy "thanks, but no thanks." But my pride, and not to mention the way my body reacts whenever he speaks, tells me to give him a chance.

Dante is no doubt a very attractive man, and even if the guy isn't gay, if being on set with him all day means I can drool over him and other random strangers, then that is good enough for me.

"Then I'm your guy," I say with a smile.

Dante's mouth curves into a smile too and I feel as if a weight has been lifted off my shoulders.

"What do you say we get back out there, finish our breakfast, and enjoy the sights of Sydney Harbour?"

"Sounds like a plan."

We head back to the table, and I take a seat next to Steve, while Dante takes the seat on my other side. We don't say much through breakfast, though the production crew and Dante discuss several topics regarding the show, things like weather conditions, shooting locations, and that's when I remember the conversation I had with Kate before I left home.

"Dante, where exactly are we staying during the show? In *The Bachelor* they had this house and all the contestants lived there."

He finishes eating, then he looks at Steve and then me before he says, "We bought a house in Circular Quay and one in Manly, which will be the location of the show while we're filming. We're staying at the hotel until Sunday, then catching the ferry to Manly where you'll stay in the house until we wrap up. The crew and I will be staying on location."

"So it's just me and Steve in that house, the entire time?"

"Yup, except of course when we're filming. You'll have the production crew following you around."

I was used to the paparazzi taking my photos and plastering them all over billboards around LA and Manhattan. I'd been in front of the camera every week, and in millions of people's homes acting, but this, this is real life, people aren't going to see

Levi Beckett anymore, they are going to be watching me, Deacon Brady. I look at Steve as he finishes the last of his breakfast, and the sight of him sitting there, biting his lower lip, makes my cock react in a way it hasn't for a very long time. The more I stare at the guy, the hotter he gets, and the more my cock throbs at the idea of having him naked and in my bed for the next four weeks.

We finish breakfast, and Dante decides that a nice boat cruise around the harbor will be the perfect way for Steve and I to get better acquainted before the show, even though we'll most likely talk about that on our first episode. You always see the chemistry between two people when they're on stage or screen, and sometimes you have to wonder how it is that two perfect strangers get along so well together when they don't even know each other. It was like that for me and Tessa, and we ended up becoming best friends, which made our relationship on screen more realistic. She texted me the other day, wishing me all the best and success for finding more work. I can't tell her about the show yet or send her any photos of where I am, but I guess she'll find out soon enough what's been happening when it goes to air. I'll definitely be saving a bunch of photos of my travels for when I can post them on my Instagram. I guess Dante's idea of Steve and I spending some time together before the show, is a good way for the two of us to build the chemistry for the cameras.

Steve and I take a seat toward the rear of the ferry, while Dante and the rest of the crew take photographs from the bow. I take out my camera and get a great panoramic view of Sydney Harbour, and as we travel under the bridge, I look to my left and notice a huge Ferris wheel and a roller coaster.

"What is that, some sort of amusement park in the middle of the ocean?" I ask Steve.

"That's Luna Park. It's full of rides and games for kids and adults of all ages. There's one in Melbourne too, and they're very popular, especially on weekends and holidays."

"And you have it in the middle of the ocean?" I ask.

"Not exactly. It's on a pier that leads out onto the harbor but you're not exactly floating in the middle of the water. I can assure you, you're on solid ground."

As the ferry drifts past the amusement park, I notice the huge, scary looking face.

"What's with the face?" I ask.

"That's the entrance to the park. That's what makes it famous."

"The scary clown face makes it famous? God, you guys are so weird down here."

Steve chuckles and I turn my attention to him. "What's so funny?" I ask.

"Nothing, but I have a confession to make."

"What's that?"

"Please don't take this the wrong way or anything, but you have the hottest accent."

"Well, if I'm being honest also, I absolutely love the way your accent rolls off your tongue."

Jesus, did I just fucking say that out loud?

"I, ah, I mean…"

I've known the guy all of five minutes and what, I'm already flirting with him?

"It's okay. You can just keep talking. I could sit here all day and listen to you."

"Don't you watch American shows?" I ask.

"Constantly. But hearing an American accent in real life is different. And to be honest, it does sound hot hearing it out of your mouth in real life, Levi Beckett."

Fuck me. Is he flirting with me? Has he been told to say that? Are we meant to be acting right now?

"Jesus, I haven't been addressed as Levi for so long, I'd almost forgotten the guy even existed."

"Levi was… kind of hot. I mean, not that I'm saying you're not hot, it's just… ah fuck, I'll just shut up and die now."

He turns away and looks out at the water. I can't help but laugh.

"There's nothing to be embarrassed about, I get it. You think I'm attractive. I can't tell you how often people told me that on a daily basis when I used to live in Los Angeles."

"Lived?"

"It's a very long story, but I moved back to New York with my parents before I was offered this job."

I know there'll be more questions he'll want answers to, so I figure, the less I tell him now, the more we get to talk about during the show. After all, it *is* a reality TV show about love and finding "the one," and I don't know, but something inside lights up whenever I speak to this guy, something I haven't felt since … Brodie.

It's a few hours later when we finish touring the harbor and arrive at Manly beach. We step off the ferry, and as we make our way to the main road, I notice Zac's car ahead. Behind it are two other black cars. Zac steps out of the first vehicle and makes his way to the opposite side of the car and opens the door.

"Deacon, you and Steve will go with Zac. The crew and I will follow in the other cars."

Without another word, Dante and the production crew, whose names I don't remember, make their way to the other cars and sit inside, while Steve and I head toward Zac.

"Welcome, Steve. My name is Zac, I'll be your driver for the next few weeks."

"Holy shit, I have a driver?"

"*We* have a driver," I correct. "Apparently, according to Dante, Zac will take us wherever we need to go, anytime, during the taping of the show."

We make ourselves comfortable, as Zac gets into the driver's seat and pulls out onto the road. I look out the back window and see the other two cars following us.

TITLE: Tainted Love
DIRECTOR: Six - Steve

*M*onday morning, and it's our first day of shooting *Tainted Love*. The past few days with Deacon Brady have been … interesting, to say the least. Meeting him in person, certainly wasn't what I was expecting at all. Aside from the fact that he is sexy as fuck in real life, I am actually going to be spending the next four weeks alone with him in this huge-ass house. The guy was delicious on TV, but in real life, he is a pure fucking sex God.

Dante informed us that we both needed to be ready for filming at 7:00 a.m. sharp. Thankfully, my day job requires me to be up at four thirty in the morning, so early mornings aren't a problem for me. Deacon on the other hand, that is an entirely different story. I finish my shower and head out into the living room of the four-bedroom, two-bathroom house Deacon and I will be spending the next month in. I walk toward his wide-open bedroom door, and as I look inside, I find Deacon isn't in his bed. As I make my way through the rest of the house, I hear the water running in the bathroom. I head to the kitchen and prepare breakfast, making enough for Deacon to eat when he gets out of the shower.

"Morning."

I turn around to see Deacon standing behind me in nothing but a towel, the water still dripping down his face and chest, and steam coming off his body.

"M-morning," I stutter, trying to stop my eyes from wandering the length of his body.

"You okay?" he asks.

"Yep, I'm fine. Considering I'm standing in a strange house with the one and only Deacon Brady."

"Do you really have to say it like that?"

"Like what? It's the truth, everyone knows you, and that's why you're going to be great on this show. I'm just Steve, the one that nobody knows anything about."

Okay, so maybe I'm telling this guy way too much. We are about to start shooting in a couple of hours, and all I can think about is seeing this guy naked.

"I guess that's what this show is all about, meeting new people, and introducing you to the rest of the world."

"But I've never done anything like this before. You're used to being in front of the camera and acting with total strangers. This is a first for me."

"You're overthinking it, Steve. You have to go out there and just be yourself. No one's expecting you to be something, or someone that you're not. The show is about love and finding me a bachelor. You've got to make the viewers believe we're falling in love because that's what's going to get us the ratings. Trust me, I know."

He sounds so casual, like he knows exactly what he's talking about, which really shouldn't surprise me considering he's done this as a living for years. I grab the plate of eggs and place it on the table in the center of the room. Deacon sits down on the chair opposite me and we eat our breakfast without saying much more to one another.

I hear my phone vibrate on the counter behind me, and reach for it to check the message.

DANTE: Shooting starts in one hour. Meet by the pool.

OK. Just finishing breakfast. I text my reply.

I make my way back to the table and sit down.
"Everything okay?"
"Yeah, just Dante telling us to meet at the pool in an hour. You know what I've always wondered?"
"What's that?" Deacon asks.
"If these shows are scripted? I mean, do you really think the contestants say half the shit they do? Or do you think it's just scripted for the ratings?"
"I guess we'll find out soon enough."
I watch as he stands and walks past me, heading for the bedroom. My eyes can't help but wander to the lower part of his body as I watch his ass cheeks flex under the towel.
What the hell are you doing, Steve? You don't even know the guy.
I head to my room, where I find Danni, the woman I'd been introduced to as our wardrobe assistant, standing by the bed with a make-up bag, a brush, and some other fancy looking stuff. I walk over to her and smile. "Hi, Danni."

"Good morning, Steve. Are you ready for the show?"

"Kind of nervous, actually, but other than that, yeah, I'm good to go."

"Perfect. Okay, I've chosen these clothes for you, when you're done, sing out and I'll come back and glam you up."

She walks out of the room, and I look down at the pile of clothing she's left me on the bed. With the warm weather showing no signs of changing for at least the next few days, I'm thankful Danni has accommodated for the heat. Calvin Klein board shorts, a white Hugo Boss T-shirt, and as I look down at the floor, I notice a pair of Havaianas thongs. I quickly change into the outfit that was chosen for me and call out to Danni.

I spend the next half hour in hair and make-up and after checking myself out in the mirror, I have to admit, I look pretty damn hot. I'd never worn make-up before, and I could never afford to buy this style of clothing. As I stare at my reflection, I wonder what Deacon looks like all glammed up. I don't have to wait long however, because I hear Lauren, the show runner, call from outside the bathroom, alerting me that we'll be shooting in five minutes.

I make my way through the living room to one of the doors next to the kitchen, and as I slide the door open, Danni adjusts what limited hair I have on my head, and touches up the already perfect make-up she'd applied only minutes earlier. As I walk through the open door, I see Dante standing there, looking at me and he gives me a wolf whistle.

"Damn. You look great, Steve."

"Thanks." I blush. "What about Deacon? How does he look?"

"Why don't you find out for yourself." He stretches out his hand, gesturing for me to walk forward, and as I do, I see

Deacon, standing by the pool. He's wearing black board shorts, a white T-shirt, his hair is evenly parted to one side, and when I look down at his feet, I notice a pair of black sandals.

There's certainly no mistaking it, the guy is fucking spectacular. I have no idea what the expectations of this show are, but judging by the way he's standing there and looking at me from the pool, I can tell it is going to be one hell of a fight to try and contain myself and keep my hands off this guy for an entire month. I walk closer to him until we're both standing only a few inches apart.

"I hope you don't expect me to give you a rose, because I so don't do that shit," Deacon jokes.

"Of course not. I wouldn't want you to ruin your reputation."

"Camera's rolling in five … four … three …," Derek the camera guy informs us, giving the 'two' and 'one' as fingers counting down.

This show is all about ratings, so I do the one thing I think will really give the audience something to talk about, and no doubt, something that will probably give me a raging hard-on. I lean forward and press my lips to Deacon's in a stolen kiss.

It's kind of weird, having people follow Deacon and I around for nine hours a day. Whenever the lighting doesn't look right, or the wind changes suddenly, Danni's quick to touch up our make-up. There are times when I forget that we're on a reality show, and whenever I try to get Deacon alone, Derek suddenly appears and zooms in on us with his camera. There aren't any scripts, but Dante knows what the people want, or maybe it's what *he* wants. There are several moments where Dante instructs Deacon and I to get closer, press our bodies together, kiss. You name it, Dante pretty much wants us to do it all. Not that I am complaining one little bit; being this close to Deacon Brady, is like a fucking dream come true.

The guy is pure fucking perfection. Perfectly put together in every single way, and the more time I spend with him, the more I want to be with him. I know I'm only the first bachelor he'll meet, and there are still eleven more countries he'll travel to before he chooses his man. While he's here with me, and there are no limitations when the cameras stop rolling, I intend to do whatever the fuck it takes to make sure he never forgets me.

"You know, the more time I spend with you and listen to you talk, the more I fall in love with your accent," I hear Deacon say as he grabs a piece of fruit from the bowl resting in the center of the table.

"Just my accent?" I question, with a cheeky grin.

I look up and see Derek zoom in closer, and I know he wants us to kiss, or do something. We've been in this house for three days now, and so far all we've managed to do is talk, get to know one another, eat, and swim in this huge-assed pool while the cameras roll. But when the cameras turn off at night, that's when the heat really turns up. I haven't slept with the guy, but it isn't for lack of trying, but I have, on several occasions, caught Deacon walking out of the shower with nothing but a towel wrapped around his waist. The sight inflates my cock, which throbs every time I go near the guy whenever he's like that.

By the time we wrap up shooting for the day, it is almost seven. Lauren organizes dinner for Deacon and I before heading off somewhere, no doubt to join the rest of the crew for dinner.

"I think I'm kind of getting the hang of this," I say, sitting down on the couch in front of the TV.

"What's that?"

"This. The whole being followed around, no privacy. Being with you, knowing that the world is watching."

"I did say you'd get used to it." He smiles.

I can feel the heat between us, and I desperately want to throw myself on top of the guy, kiss his fucking brains out, and do God only knows what else. But I don't want to freak the guy out and have a reputation on this show as a whore, but Jesus… this is Deacon fucking Brady.

"You're awfully quiet," I hear him say.

"I'm just thinking," I reply.

"Oh, about what?"

"It doesn't matter. It's not appropriate anyway."

"What's not appropriate?" he asks.

"These thoughts that I'm having. I mean, I don't know you that well. We've only been shooting this show and living in this house for a few days, yet I've watched you for years and I know you must get this a lot, but I can't stop looking at you and noticing how gorgeous you are."

"Yeah, I do get that a lot."

I feel my pulse speed up, and my entire body tightens, like I'm waiting for some tidal wave, or a volcanic eruption to occur. There's no one else around, it's just Deacon and I. No Dante telling us what to do, no cameras, just us.

"Can… Is it okay …?" I can't even find the words to finish my sentence. I focus my gaze on Deacon, but it's obvious my words aren't needed. He leans forward and as I close my eyes, I feel his lips press against mine.

Now this, *this* is what a real kiss fucking feels like. His tongue intertwines with mine, and as I lean my head back, my mouth parts as he kisses down my neck and licks my Adam's apple. He continues his journey down my neck, stopping at the opening of the T-shirt I'm wearing. He pulls himself back and lifts the shirt over my head, throwing it on the floor before removing his own to join mine.

Muscle upon muscle. That is the only way to describe Deacon Brady, the Sexiest Man Alive, and here he is, completely shirtless next to me. He leans forward and presses his lips against my shoulder, pushing me down onto the couch until he's lying on top of me. I place a palm on his chest and tap my fingers across each of his abs. The guy is sex on a stick.

"Is it true what they say about you Australians?" he asks.

"What's that?" I enquire.

"That all you Aussie men have huge cocks?"

Okay, so, not what I was expecting him to ask, but since he's asked the question, I figure it's only polite to answer. "Why don't you take me into the bedroom… and find out."

What? Am I seriously going to give up the opportunity with this guy? Hell no. Especially considering the fact my cock has just gone from subtle, to rock fucking hard.

Deacon stands and heads toward his bedroom, so I pull myself off the couch and follow. Once safely inside his room, I kick the door closed and lock it.

TITLE: Tainted Love

DIRECTOR: Seven - Deacon

*J*esus Christ. This is not what I thought would happen during my first week of shooting. But seriously, this guy, his charm, personality, that body, and his accent, how the hell am I supposed to resist all that. Thanks to my years of having a personal trainer, I'm ripped, damn ripped. But Steve, this guy is something else. I've seen the way he's looked at me on set all week; the lust in his eyes and his body screaming 'fuck me.' It's hard to believe this guy has completely blown my mind in only a few short days, since it took Brodie and I almost two months before we agreed to make our relationship official and then another two weeks after that before we slept together.

Is it even possible to feel this way about someone I've only known for less than a week? I'm not the type to just jump in bed and screw a guy, but we've spent every single day together and I've learned a lot about him. He had a troubled childhood, and it really sounded like the guy was just trying to have a second chance. Maybe that's why I'm so drawn to him. With Steve, everything feels different. Maybe it's because I know that in less than a month, I'll probably never see the guy again. But what is it about him that draws me to him? I have no idea. Looking at him now though with his hair slicked back, and the fake tan on his body, thanks to Danni, the guy is all sexed up.

I watch as Steve makes his way over to the bed I've been sleeping in for the past few days. Not wasting any time, I wander over there and sit down beside him, taking his mouth in a brutal kiss. My pulse speeds up and I can feel my cock throb beneath the confines of the denim, and tonight, thanks to my older, somewhat dirty, perverted sister for insisting I pack some lube and condoms, I intend to use it to its full potential, with Steve. I unzip my jeans and throw them to the floor, before removing my own underwear, as I watch Steve do the same with his shorts. I kiss my way down his neck and as I get to my knees, my tongue travels down his abs and to his well-defined V, I can smell his arousal.

"Let's see if the theory is correct," I say, grabbing the top of his underwear and sliding it down his thighs.

I can hear him moan above me as my lips run lower and lower until I'm only inches from his throbbing cock, which is practically dripping with pre-cum.

"Holy shit, that *is* a big boy," I say.

"You better believe it, just over nine inches."

"Nine inches, huh? Well, let's see how this nine-inch flesh feels between my lips."

I open my mouth and place it over the head of Steve's swollen dick and begin worshiping the thick piece of meat, sliding it in and out of my mouth. I feel a firm pair of hands press against the back of my head, guiding it, as I lick up and down the throbbing length.

"How does that feel?" I ask.

"Fucking amazing, I've had plenty of— Oh Jesus."

The way his voice sounds when he curses is enough to make me almost come early. I continue to swallow him whole, taking him deeper to the back of my throat. I grab my own cock, jacking myself off as my hand works my own throbbing dick. Steve's cock is slick now, making it easier for it to slide in and out of my mouth. With each muffled groan coming from Steve's mouth, I stroke my length harder and faster, but I don't want to come yet, not before I've had a proper taste of this guy. I stop stroking myself and pull my lips from his cock. I kiss my way up his stomach and chest before my mouth finally finds his again. I pull him until he's standing up, then drop back onto my knees. I place my hands on each of his ass cheeks and slap them as I continue to mouth fuck his cock, and I hear Steve grunt with pleasure.

"Your ass is so fucking firm. I could stay here all night and torment the fuck out of it."

"Well, we're not exactly going anywhere, and there are no cameras around."

I'm pretty sure that's an invitation to do whatever the fuck I want. As I stand, my erection presses against his skin, and I feel him wrap a fist around both our cocks. I can't stop touching the guy, which is going to make things difficult in a few weeks when I have to say goodbye and head to God knows where. What are the chances of ever seeing him again? Dante made it pretty clear that I'm not allowed to fall in love, or I risk losing the twelve million. Okay, so I wasn't in love with the guy, but the more I touched him, the more I tasted him, and the more I wanted him, the more I found myself needing him. But I don't want to just fuck this guy and have it over with, I'm not that type of guy.

"As tempting as that offer is, I don't want to be known as the guy who fucked over Steve …" It suddenly occurs to me that I don't know a vital piece of information. "Sorry, I don't even know your last name."

"Um … funny you should say that."

"What's so funny about that?"

"Beckett."

"Why is Beckett funny?" I ask, not entirely sure if he is mocking my on-screen name or if he is trying to tease me by calling me that.

"Beckett is my surname, or last name as you call it."

"No fucking way. Are you shitting me?" I ask.

"Not at all. I think that was one of the reasons why I was so fascinated with you. Not just because of how hot you are, but also because we share the same last name. Well, on screen for you at least."

That makes me chuckle a little. Levi Beckett was a part of my life for a long time, and I guess he had an impact on everyone. But he's not a part of me anymore, and I don't want the world, or Steve, remembering me as him. I look at the man who has captured my heart over the last few days, and I really take in everything I possibly can. I really want this guy, and it is obvious from his growing arousal that he wants me too. Forget that I'm here in this strange place, with these total strangers and just totally go with it. But I have more respect than that, and I'm not about to use this guy for sex.

"I'm sorry, did I freak you out?" I hear him ask.

"No, not at all. Just hearing it from you is different."

"Different, how?"

"I don't know. I can't explain it. We don't know each other that well, you know. We've been here less than a week, the cameras have been rolling and following our every move, and we haven't even had a proper opportunity to explore."

"Um … what would you call this?" he says, grabbing my cock and squeezing it in his palm.

"Holy Jesus fucking Christ."

"I've fantasized about this since the moment I saw you on television. I would rip your photo out of the magazine, pin it up on the back of my bedroom door and jerk off to it every night before I went to bed. Then, when I found out they were making a reality show solely with gay men, I just had to audition. Of course, I didn't ever think I'd make it, much less get a call back. Then there's the bonus of meeting you."

He continues to fist my cock softly, and I wrap my arms around his waist, pulling him in toward me.

"Then what happened?"

"Once the producers notified me, they told me that we'd start filming in January, and they'd fly me from Melbourne to be here where I'd need to live for a month, all expenses paid. To be honest, when I found out I'd made it, I thought it was a joke up until the time I was on a plane to Sydney."

I feel my entire body go taut; I don't want to fuck this guy, not yet, but with his body pressed against mine, I'm finding it more and more difficult to contain my urge.

Steve leans forward and presses his lips against my naked shoulder. With one hand, he continues to torment my cock, and with the other, he traces the outline of my defined V and all of a sudden, I feel a pair of hard teeth bite down on my soft flesh.

"*Ah,* what the fuck?"

"Sorry, you have an incredible body, and you're just so fucking hot," he whispers.

"Thank you," are the only words I manage to say.

I look over at the clock beside the bed, and my eyes widen when I realize it's almost three in the morning.

"We've got to be up in less than four hours for shooting."

I hear the disappointed groan escape his lips and he releases his grip on my cock.

"I know this is going to sound completely nuts, but all I've been thinking about tonight, since we got back here, is how much I really want to fuck you."

I guess I'd seen it coming all week because if I'm being honest, it's the only thing that's been on my mind too. But as I hear the words come out of his mouth, I physically cease to function and comprehend anything else. His hands stop worshipping my cock, instead traveling the length of my body, tormenting me all over.

"I've just come out of a pretty fucked-up relationship."

I want to kick myself in the ass for what I just said, but I really want to be honest with this guy. I watch as he pulls away and sits down on the bed, and even in the dark, I can see the slight disappointment in his eyes.

"It's nothing personal. Like I said, I just got out of a really bad relationship. The last thing I want is to get hurt, and more importantly, hurt anyone else who's with me."

"I'm so sorry, I …"

"You don't need to apologize. I'm just not ready for that type of commitment again, not yet, especially when—"

My words trail off and I sit there staring at the man beside me.

Don't, Brady. Don't let yourself fall in love with this guy.

"I'm sorry, I wasn't thinking."

I place his face between my palms and I pull him toward me. I bring our lips together in a fiery kiss.

"Why don't you stay with me tonight? I'd really like to know what it feels like to have my cock between *your* lips."

TITLE: Tainted Love

DIRECTOR: Eight - Steve

*I*f it was physically possible to have your heart skip a million beats and still function, then it appears to have happened to me. I can feel my chest rise with each labored breath, but I never take my eyes off the man sitting beside me for even a brief second. I lean forward and push my tongue between his lips in a heated kiss. I can feel his entire body, and mine, vibrate from the connection of our lips. Our tongues meet in combat, and it's a game of tongue tangling war. His tongue feels amazing in my mouth, but what would be more amazing, is to know what it feels like to have his cock shoved between my lips. There is nothing I can do to settle the throbbing shaft that's brushing against my own skin as I continue to worship Deacon's mouth. I feel him pull away as our lips part.

"Wow, holy shit."

"What?" I ask.

"I think you just kissed my fucking brains out. No one's ever kissed me like that before," I hear him say.

"I'm going to assume you're not complaining, because if you are, you better move away, let me get the fuck out of here and to my own room so that I can stop myself from doing what I really want."

"No, I'm not complaining. And what exactly do you want to do to me?"

"I really wanna suck your cock," I confess.

"Well, that's pretty forward."

"I'm being honest. Will you deny me the honor of hardcore foreplay?"

"Hardcore foreplay?"

"Mhmm. Why don't you let me show you what I mean."

I press my mouth to his once more and bite down on Deacon's lower lip, and as I pull away, I hear him curse with pain, but that doesn't deter me from where I want to go. Maneuvering him backward, I press his body against the hard wall, and I continue kissing my way across his cheek, down his neck, and I slide my tongue across his protruding Adam's apple. Going lower, my lips mold to the soft skin, as inch by inch, muscle by muscle, I continue my trail down this sexual highway until I'm only inches away from his rigid length. I can smell his arousal, and as I lower my lips, I look up at the man above me. His eyes are closed, and I know from the way he's bucking his hips forward, that he's ready for me to take him. I wrap my fist around his shaft and gently tug at the hard length as I lick the tip of the head.

"Oh, fuck yes," I hear him moan as I take another lick of the swollen head.

I hold onto his leg with one hand, while I squeeze his balls with my other. I fasten my lips around the object of my desire that has my cock screaming, and swallow Deacon's length to the back of my throat. I shut my eyes, and I can feel Deacon push farther into my mouth, shoving himself in and out with deep, hard thrusts.

"Holy fucking shit, you're amazing at this," Deacon pants, as I continue to take him deeper down my throat.

Two firm hands press against the back of my head and with each thrust of Deacon's hips, he manages to push his cock deeper, if that is even remotely possible. His arousal is evident as I taste the salty fluid on my tongue, but I'm not ready for him to come, no, this isn't over yet. I feel my own erection pound painfully in rhythm with Deacon's cock sliding between my lips, so I reach down to palm myself, speeding up the pace, as I allow my fist to go full throttle up and down my veiny length. Not wanting to come before I've had the chance to properly taste him, I spread my palms across his thighs, until my fingers reach the root of his shaft.

The guy's cock is beautifully cut. Yeah sure, I was cut, and at just over nine inches, I thought that was pretty damn impressive. But the way Deacon's cock throbs inside my mouth, screams pure fucking perfection on every count, from length to how hard it is. A harsh curse escapes his lips, and I know that any moment now, Deacon will be ready to blow his load, and when he does, I want to taste every bit of him.

I continue lubricating his shaft with my saliva-slickened tongue as I validate my delight a little while longer. Deciding to concentrate on a more sensitive area, I grab one of his nipples and massage it between my thumb and forefinger, and I hear another moan escape his lips.

"You're so fucking good at this, I swear to God, I don't think I'm going to last much longer if you keep doing that."

"I'm ready for you to come, but when you do, it has to be in my mouth," I whisper.

"Do it. Do whatever it takes, I'm close."

No further invitation is needed as I travel down his body once more, until my lips are inches away from his engorged length. I place my hands on each of his ass cheeks and torment the soft skin, and before I wrap my lips around his cock, I spit on my finger, and gently insert my index finger inside him.

"Jesus," I hear him curse as he bucks his hips forward, pushing his cock deeper down my throat. I feel the delicious length swell inside my mouth, and I take the opportunity to insert another digit. That has Deacon moaning louder, and as he continues to thrust in and out of me, I begin stroking my own erection.

"Come. I want us to come together," Deacon orders, and I have absolutely no problem obeying his request.

I continue stroking myself, harder and faster, and with each lick of Deacon's delicious cock, I can taste the evident pre-cum on his head. I feel his hand behind my head, pushing me down on his eager length. "Fucking suck it," he orders as I take him deeper, and deeper. As he pushes into my mouth for the final time, it's all I need and I can hear him moan with satisfaction as he comes in a hot, sticky climax down my throat.

Lowering myself onto the bed, I try and catch my breath as I spread out on the sheets. I look up and see Deacon with a wicked, satisfied grin on his face. My mouth is aching from the marathon workout it's just performed on this guy, and judging by the way Deacon is still towering over me, he is as pleased and satisfied as I am. He crawls on top of the bed and lies down beside me, placing a hand across my bare chest.

"Wow!"

"Wow? Seriously, that's it?" I tease.

"It's all I've got for now." He chuckles.

"This has certainly been a night to remember," I tell him.

"Yeah, for you and me both."

He turns to glance at the clock which reads almost four o'clock.

"You know, if we don't get some sleep, Dante's not going to be happy if we're walking around on set like something out of *The Walking Dead* instead of a reality TV show about a bachelor."

"Yeah, you're right." I yawn.

"By the way, you never told me your age," I hear him ask.

"My age? What's that got to do with anything?"

"Nothing, I'm just curious, that's all."

"Well, how old do you think I am? You think very carefully before you answer that question, Mr. Brady," I tease, rolling over to face him. I prop up on my elbow and rest my head on my palm as I brush a hand across his smooth chest.

"I'd say you can't be older than twenty-five, thirty, tops."

I look at the man and give him a sheepish grin.

"What's that look for?"

"Twenty-five, really?"

"Oh shit. Please tell me you're over eighteen?"

"Of course. I wouldn't be allowed to appear on the show if I wasn't," I confirm.

"Okay, so how old are you then?"

I place my palm on his cheek and stroke it gently, as I say, "I'm almost thirty-nine."

"Shut the fuck up," he booms, sitting up on the bed.
"What? Why is that so hard to believe?"
"There's no way you're… I mean, it's just…"
"What?" I ask.
"You don't look a day over twenty-five. Your parents must have really good genes."
"Yeah, I get that a lot, but truth be told, I'll be forty before you know it."

I notice him raise a brow, as he leans in toward me, he places a hand behind my neck and tugs me toward him, catching me completely off guard as I slip from my current position and almost face plant the bed. Our mouths meet and he crushes them together in another tormented kiss.

"We should get some sleep," he whispers as he pulls away.
"Yeah, I suppose we should," I agree.

We head to the bathroom and clean up our mess before crawling into bed naked together. It's a hot night, and I'm not just talking about the aftermath of what happened between us, so he turns up the air con and pulls the cover over both of us. He leans in toward me and places a hand over my chest as he whispers, "Goodnight, Steve," and places a kiss on my temple.

"Goodnight, Deacon," I reply as I slowly shut my eyes and drift off to sleep.

TITLE *Tainted Love*

DIRECTOR Nine - Deacon

CAMERA

DATE **SCENE** **TAKE**

*W*e're down to the final week of filming. It's the weekend and there is a lot more haze in the air, from all the fires still burning out of control. Steve, Danni, Lauren, and I, agree to go out and tour Sydney some more before we start filming again. We head toward the amusement park Steve and I had seen on my first day here. I'm not a fan of fast rides or anything really that goes more than three feet in the air. As we head inside, Danni and Lauren grab me by the arm.

"You have to come on the dodgem cars with us," Lauren pleads.

"The what?" I say.

"Oh, they mean the bumper cars, Deacon."

"Oh, gotcha."

Not being able to resist either of their pretty faces, I concede and allow Lauren to drag me over to the line for the bumper cars.

"Not joining us?" I ask Steve.

"Nah, I don't feel so great. I might give this one a miss," he says.

"Are you all right?"

"Yeah, I'm fine. Might be a bit of heat stroke from the sun."

I stare at him, not entirely sure I should leave him alone.

"I'll stay with him," Danni suggests, as she takes a seat beside Steve at the cafeteria.

"Thanks, Danni. Come on, Deacon, before the line gets too long," Lauren whines as she pulls me away toward the cars.

"You're very fond of him, aren't you?" Lauren asks.

"We've grown pretty close these past few weeks. He's a great guy."

"Yeah, he is."

"So, how long have you and Danni been friends?" I ask, quickly changing the subject to avoid another discussion that might lead to my feelings toward Steve. I have to keep reminding myself that I can't fall in love with the guy, I can't fall in love with anyone, that's not part of the deal. If I do, I can kiss goodbye the twelve million, and my chance at rebuilding my finances.

"Um, Danni is actually my partner."

"Oh, you're both gay?"

"Yes. We've known each other for years. We graduated university together, she studied make-up and I got into film, which is how I landed the part of the show runner. We started dating right after we graduated."

"Really?"

She nods and we slowly move forward in the line, almost reaching the start.

"What do you think of Australia so far?"

"Sydney's a beautiful city. It's absolutely heartbreaking what's happening at the moment with all these fires. It's made news all over the world. So tragic."

"Yeah, it's the worst it has been in many years, and unfortunately they don't see any end in sight, not unless we get some decent rainfall over the next few months."

As Lauren and I continue our discussion, we make our way onto one of the bumper cars. I look out at Steve and see that he's smiling with Danni and my heart skips a beat at the sight of the smile on his gorgeous face. The guy has really captivated my heart, and after the other night in the bedroom we agreed that that was as far as things were going to go, although we had continued with several nights of pleasurable foreplay. As much as we couldn't keep our hands off each other, I managed to convince Steve that things would get extremely awkward if we fucked, especially considering I was leaving the country in less than a week. There was also the major problem of not allowing myself to fall in love, or risk losing everything.

After riding the bumper cars, Lauren insists we ride the Ferris wheel which gives me a great panoramic, but hazy view of Sydney Harbour. It's such an incredibly beautiful city, and my heart aches for the tragic loss that the Australians have suffered. As we head off the Ferris wheel, I walk over to Steve who throws me a simple smile; it's one of the familiar traits I've come to learn about him over the past few weeks, and even though I have no clue what's going on in that beautiful head of his, I know that this is his way of telling me that he's okay... *things* between *us* are okay.

As we stroll around Luna Park, the sun shining and trying to push its rays through the hazy sky, I can really feel the heat bouncing off my T-shirt. I look to my left and see Lauren and

Danni holding hands as Danni leans in and presses her lips to Lauren. I love that the two of them can just be so casual here, and have no one around to tell them they're not allowed to fall in love. As I look to my right I see Steve, casually strolling beside me, and I feel sweat start to drip down my brow. I cross my arms over my torso and pull the T-shirt over my head. I tuck it into the back pocket of my shorts as I reach for Steve's hand and intertwine our fingers together.

"Ewww, that's totally gross, will you put your shirt back on, please," I hear Danni plea mockingly.

"Yeah, you'll scare all the chicks away," Lauren adds.

I smile at the two of them, but say nothing when I hear Steve say, "Well, I think he looks spectacular in a singlet. Hellooo biceps."

Steve smacks my arm as I turn to lock eyes with him.

"Sing ... what?"

Lauren, Danni, and Steve burst out laughing.

"What's so funny?"

"It's a singlet, mate."

"What in God's name is a singlet?" I ask, looking at the three of them, totally clueless.

"That thing that you're wearing, it's called a singlet."

"This thing?" I ask, pulling at the fabric covering my midsection.

Steve nods, as I look down at my top, then at Lauren, Danni, and finally at Steve as I state, "This is a wife beater."

A roar of laughter comes from the three of them.

"A what?" Danni asks.

"A wife beater."

"Who the hell calls a piece of clothing a wife beater? It sounds more like a vicious attacker who goes around hitting women." Lauren looks at me and frowns.

Although she's way off the mark, in some strange way, she kind of makes a valid point.

"Do I need to remind you Aussies, that you people are the ones who walk around the streets in summer with those things on your feet that … what was it my sister called them, a thong?"

Again, the three of them burst into laughter. I turn to Steve again, and he looks at me with the cutest smile on his face.

"Enjoying yourselves?"

"Thongs. They're called thongs," Steve corrects me.

"Thongs, a thong, what's the difference? It's still a piece of clothing that should not be worn on your feet but up your—"

"Yeah, thank you so much for the visual, Deacon."

"Hey, you guys are the ones that talk funny."

"Says the person who calls a singlet a wife beater."

"Point taken," I reply.

After stopping for lunch, we continue our walk through the park. I grab some souvenirs to take home with me for my parents, Kate, Thomas, and the twins when I return at the end of the year, they'll make great Christmas presents. The girls always told me how much they wanted to go to Australia, and if they couldn't come to Australia, then maybe I could take some of Australia back with me. I feel Steve's hand press against my back, and there is nothing more I want to do than be able to take him back to the house, cover him with kisses and tell him that everything is going to be fine. But I know that I'm living a fantasy; I can't possibly expect this guy to wait for me. Hell, I don't even know what's going to happen when all this is over,

Dante and I never discussed what would happen once we finished shooting *Tainted Love*.

By nightfall, we're all pretty exhausted. Danni and Lauren head back to the hotel where they are staying with the rest of the production crew, while Steve and I head back to the house. We are due on set in the morning, 7:00 a.m. sharp as per usual.

"Are you all right? You've been really quiet since we left the amusement park."

"I'm just thinking," Steve replies.

"About?"

"A lot of things. I mean, I'm no virgin, but if you'd told me three weeks ago that I'd be waking up naked in bed with Deacon Brady, I probably would have punched you in the face, or called you a liar."

"Yet here we both are," I say.

He nods but doesn't say anything else. God, I wish I could get inside the guy's head and see what's going on in there. The night is mild, and I know that unless I take a nice, soothing shower, I'm not going to get any sleep.

"I really need to take a shower."

Stepping past him, I head to the bathroom and close the door.

The warm spray feels great on my body, and it is exactly what I need to calm down and relax. Today hasn't been stressful, in fact, thanks to Danni and Lauren, it was actually quite entertaining knowing that the Australians have different meanings for words over here. As I allow the water to ooze over my soft skin, I close my eyes and think about Steve and the time we've spent together these past three weeks, knowing that in a few short days, it will all be over. I reach down and gently stroke my aching cock, wishing that Steve was down on his knees and worshipping me like the king he made me feel like.

I am going to miss him, and as that thought enters my mind, I wonder.... *Is this what it's going to be like every time I leave? Is this how I'm going to react every single time I have to say goodbye to everyone I meet?*

With my head full of thoughts, I turn off the water, and grab the towel that's hanging over the shower door. Sliding the door open, I wrap the towel around my waist and head back out to the bedroom, expecting to find Steve still sitting on the bed where I'd left him, but instead, my stomach flips as I realize he's no longer in the room.

Unwrapping the towel, I allow my now throbbing cock to spring free, and I wipe my damp hair with the towel, before placing it on the towel rack. Walking toward the bed, I notice a small piece of paper with neat handwriting. I turn on the lamp on the nightstand and bring the paper closer.

Sorry, I was really tired and started falling asleep. I wasn't sure how long you were going to be, so I decided to head back to my own bed.
Thank you for a fun day.
I'll see you on set tomorrow.

Love, Steve xx

Those two little words make my entire body vibrate, including my still hard-as-a-rock cock. I crawl into bed and turn out the light, pulling the covers up to my chin as the cool air from the AC blows in my face. I turn to my side and stare at the closed door to Steve's room, and as my cock slowly starts to subside, I feel a rush of emotion travel through me. With the gentle sound of AC, I close my eyes and slowly drift off to sleep.

Ten - Steve

Tainted Love

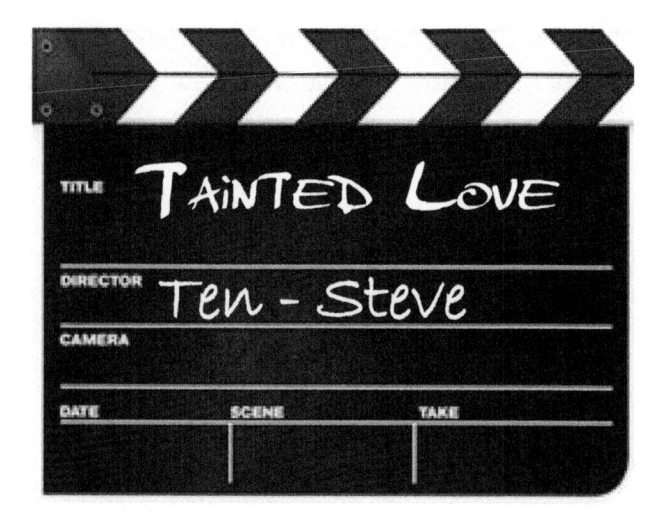

*W*ith only three days left of filming *Tainted Love,* my emotions are riding high. Deacon and I have spent every single day and night together, and the more either of us thinks about the end of the show, and our time together, the more depressed we both become. We don't want to think about it, so we both keep busy seeing more sights of Sydney and the Harbor. I sit down on the bed, looking at the wardrobe Danni has appropriately chosen for the episode today: a black tux, blue shirt, pink tie, and black dress boots.

I carefully change into the outfit, and I'm making my way to the bathroom when I hear a knock on the door. I pull the door open and see Deacon standing on the other side. He is dressed in a tux of his own, almost identical to mine. The guy is pure sex perfection and hot as hell dressed in that attire. As I raise my gaze, the heated connection we share has me leaning forward and pressing a kiss to his mouth.

"What's that for?" he asks.

"To let you know that I approve of this outfit, and also how incredibly sexy you look right now."

I place a hand on his cheek, and he tilts his head to the side.

"Do not mess with the hair. It took me all morning to perfect it."

Deacon turns around, and I look over his shoulder to see Danni walking toward us in a panic with her make-up bag, phone, and brushes.

"If you ruin my hard work, I swear I will kill both of you," she pants as she reaches the door and steps inside.

"Deacon, *you* need to get out of here so I can beautify Mr. Pedantic over here and have him ready in time to be on set."

"Pedantic, I'm not—"

"Oh, yes you are," Deacon cuts in. "But I *do* need to speak with Dante before we start filming, so I'll see you in a couple of hours."

He leans forward and places a kiss on my cheek before turning and walking out the door.

"You two are like a couple of love-sick puppies. I see the fire in both your eyes whenever you're together."

"You do, do you?" I ask.

"You can't deny that you're attracted to the guy, Steve."

"I'm not denying anything. But this is a reality show, Danni, nothing can ever happen between Deacon and me, nothing."

"Um… that's kind of the whole point of this show, isn't it? To find your Mr. Right? Otherwise, what the hell are you doing here?"

"There's still eleven more countries, which means eleven more men who will each spend time with Deacon. Any one of them could steal his heart."

"Yeah, and *you* could very well be one of those men," Danni states, as she closes the door and ushers me into the bathroom.

"Look, this whole thing is really complicated. I think we just need to chill and see what happens once the show is over."

An hour later, Danni finishes my hair and make-up, and I am finally alone and free from any more of her questions. The simple fact is that no matter how hard I try, I can't get Deacon Brady out of my mind. The more time I spend with the guy, the more I want him, and I know that I can't have him.

I never did the whole dating thing. Normally I'd go on Grindr, find some hot, random guy, take him home to my place, and fuck his brains out, before he leaves the following morning. I didn't want to set myself up for heartache. But as I sit there, in the recliner by the window looking out onto the pool, I know that Deacon Brady has changed the dynamic of things for me. My own thoughts paralyze me, until I hear Dante's voice call from outside.

"Steve?"

"I'm in here," I say, standing from the recliner and walking over to the door.

"Are you ready?"

"Where's Deacon?" I ask.

"Heading to the pool as we speak."

With a smile, I quickly adjust my tux and make my way outside the house and toward the pool where I see Deacon approaching. Dante gives us both a brief pep talk about what to expect in the scene, and while he doesn't want us to have our hands all over each other, he wants us to look sexy.

How the fuck am I supposed to look tempting with Deacon standing beside me, when everything about the guy is tempting?

Danni wanders over to us and places two roses on each of the outdoor lounge chairs resting by the pool before Dante yells, "Action."

The cameras start rolling and Deacon wraps an arm around me, pulling me in closer to him. I feel my cock spring to life in an instant, as it brushes against the material of my underwear inside my pants, and I have to wonder exactly how much the camera captures, and how much will be edited in post-production.

We spend an entire eight hours of filming talking about our expectations, what we both want in our lives, and if either of us is ready to settle down and start a family once this is over. Sitting on the lounge chair, Deacon brings the glass of champagne to his lips and takes a sip. I look over his shoulder and see Dante's head buried behind the camera, clearly happy with what is unfolding in front of him. As I lock eyes with the man sitting to my left, something occurs to me; Deacon and I really only had one on-screen kiss. He's given me a light peck on the cheek from time to time whenever Dante requested it, but neither of us has kissed the other, properly, like a *real* kiss.

Dante mentioned that *Tainted Love* was going to be different from every other reality show out there, though he hadn't mentioned how, other than the fact it was a gay version. Taking a sip of my own champagne, I smile at Deacon and lean forward as I press my lips to his. My eyes are closed, so I can't see if Dante is still recording, but the fact that he hasn't yelled "Cut" or that Deacon hasn't pushed me away, is a good indication that he is happy with what we are doing. I'm not sure how explicit this show is meant to be, or what time the show will air, but I'm pretty sure if they want it tame, they'll edit everything else out. It's hard, trying to contain myself from tearing off Deacon's clothes and running my hands all over his silky, toned body, but the cameras are rolling, and I have to remind myself that this is a reality show, and not a porno.

For our final scene of the day, Deacon and I are required to exchange a rose. By doing so, we pledge our love and commitment for one another, which is kind of backward really, considering I'm only the first contestant.

"Steve, will you accept this rose as a pledge of my commitment to you?"

I reply with the scripted words as he stretches out his hand and hands me the flower before leaning forward and kissing me on the cheek.

"I thought you 'don't do this rose shit,'" I whisper in his ear, mimicking Deacon's earlier statement when we first started shooting.

"For you, I'll make an exception."

I reach down and pick up the rose resting on the seat beside me. I look at Deacon as he focuses his gaze on me.

I repeat the question Deacon asked me as I hold the long-stemmed rose in my hands. "Steve, I accept your rose as a pledge of your commitment to me."

I lean forward and hand him the rose as I gently press a kiss to his cheek. I feel his breath on my neck as he leans into my ear and whispers, "Tonight, when the cameras stop rolling, I'm going to peel you out of that tux, piece by piece, and do all sorts of indecent things to you."

My cock throbs at the guy's promise of seduction, and I silently curse under my breath at the fact that I can't rip the goddamn tux off him now and perform my own indecent acts on him. But with the cameras still rolling, Deacon and I smile as we pull away from each other and sit down on the outdoor couch by the pool.

"Cut," Dante yells as Deacon and I finish shooting our final ever scene of *Tainted Love*. We had to get our hair fixed and make-up re-applied constantly throughout the final scene to maintain optical continuity, and we probably exchanged more than twenty roses by the time Dante was happy with the final take.

"That was by far my favorite scene with you two. You guys have such wonderful chemistry. And as for your kissing scenes, I don't know about either of you, but from where I was standing, it was pretty steamy, and I know the viewers will think so too."

There is no way this guy is straight. It's one thing to be directing behind a camera and watch us 'act,' but to deliver a compliment so confidently like he just had, wouldn't be as easy for a straight guy.

"Good job, you two. Australia is definitely going to love you, Deacon Brady, and Steve." He leans forward and gives us both a gentle pat on the back.

"So that's it, it's all over?" I ask.

"That's it! You're both free to do whatever you like. Zac will be back here at 4:00 a.m. Sunday morning to take you both to the airport."

"Thank you, Dante. This has been an incredible experience, one that I will never forget. It's been an absolute honor meeting and working with you, and I'm so grateful that I got the opportunity to be a contestant on your debut show."

I stretch out my hand for him to shake, and as he reaches out to grab it, he pulls me forward and says, "Steve, it's been an honor and a privilege having you on my show, and you've been an absolute delight." He pulls away and looks at Deacon as he continues, "You two are great together, and no matter how this turns out, I hope you both find the love and happiness you're looking for."

I choke up, and I feel my eyes begin to water, but I take a deep breath to contain my emotions. I turn to my left and look at Deacon, whose eyes have also welled up. Dante pulls him in for a tight embrace and with one final look at the two of us, he turns and walks away, leaving me alone with Deacon.

We head inside the house, and as I walk toward my room, I hear Deacon call out to me, "Seeing as it's our final few nights together, how about I cook some dinner?"

"You cook?"

"Yes. I cook. I clean. I wash. I sew. You can learn a lot when you watch daytime television. Plus, Mom taught us a lot too."

I look at the man who has completely shocked me with his domestic skills and I smile, "Wouldn't you rather call Lauren from catering and have her bring us something instead of slaving over a hot stove?"

"Well, technically … we're not filming anymore, so Lauren isn't required to bring us anything. The crew has already packed everything. And secondly—" He unclips the button on his jacket, sliding it off his shoulders and tossing it over the couch. He then pulls the shirt out of the waistband of his pants and slowly begins undoing the buttons, one by one, but his eyes stay locked with mine. I can't help but notice him wet his lips as he continues unbuttoning the shirt until he reaches the last one. He slides the shirt off his back and tosses it on the couch with the jacket before he unbuckles his belt and unzips the pants he's wearing. "—wouldn't you rather *me* naked over a hot stove?"

My cock immediately takes notice of the words coming out of his mouth, and the sight of his naked torso. I reach my hand down and slowly start rubbing my painfully aching cock. Deacon walks toward me and tugs at my shirt, unclipping the buttons piece by piece as he pulls the shirt out of my pants. He leans forward and presses his lips to mine, before making his way down my neck and sliding the shirt off my back. I let out a moan as I continue the friction on my raging hard-on.

Deacon presses his palm on my chest and unzips my pants, pushing them down my thighs and onto the floor. I feel his fingers tug at the fabric of my underwear. "I really need you to suck my cock, *now*," I hiss.

"Your cock will taste better after dinner when I devour it for dessert. So why don't *you* get out of that suit and let *me* get on with dinner so that we can both eat and then get naked."

My cock rises to full mast, pointing in his direction. I head to the bedroom and quickly change, leaving Deacon in the kitchen to prepare dinner.

It's after midnight before Deacon and I clean up the kitchen and pack our suitcases. Two more days; that's all the two of us have left before I head back home to Melbourne and back to the reality of working. I'm not sure if I will even see this guy ever again, and that thought puts a knot in the pit of my stomach. The last month with Deacon has been amazing, and contained some of the best moments of my life. As I sit on the bed, I pick up my phone from the nightstand and scroll through the photos of me and Deacon, and the memories we've made here in Sydney. It's going to be hard returning to my normal life and not being able to see or touch the man who's captivated my heart over the summer.

"What are you thinking about?" Deacon's voice cuts through my thoughts.

"Us, and how amazing the last month has been. I can't believe it's all over."

"Well, it doesn't have to be."

"What do you mean?" I ask.

"We can Skype, FaceTime, Facebook video, Snapchat, all that sort of stuff. I don't think there's anything in my contract that states we can't keep in touch. Just because I'm not here, doesn't mean we can't still communicate."

"It's not the same though as having you here," I say, crawling into the bed next to him.

"Let's not think about that now, and focus on the time we have left together in this huge-ass house that we have all to ourselves."

I nuzzle my head into his and place my lips onto Deacon's neck and kiss the Adam's apple I've become obsessed with all summer.

"You have no fucking idea how much that turns me on," I hear Deacon whisper as his lips meet mine.

"Why don't you show me just how much it turns you on?" I request.

He gives me a wicked grin, before crawling on top of me and pulling up the covers.

TITLE: *Tainted Love*

DIRECTOR: Epilogue - Deacon

I hate goodbyes. Even when Kate moved to Chicago, which was only a four-hour flight, I felt like I was saying goodbye to my best friend. Australia has indeed lived up to my every expectation. Sydney is such a beautiful and colorful city, and although the country is in a major state of crisis right now, I know that the community will rebuild again. I have some very fond memories, memories I know I will never forget, no matter what happens. Lauren and Danni came by the house early this morning to say goodbye before they both headed back home. Steve's flight to Melbourne is leaving in just over four hours, and as I wait for Dante, I turn to face the man sitting beside me.

"Are you all set?" I ask.

"Yeah, pretty much."

"You're awfully quiet."

"I just can't believe it's all over, and in a few short hours I'll be on the plane back home to Melbourne and you'll be on a plane to … wait, where exactly *are* you headed next?" he asks.

It suddenly occurs to me that I have absolutely no idea where I am going. Dante told me to be here at 5:00 a.m. sharp, and he'd meet me here.

"Um … I actually don't know. Dante told me I'd find out all the details when I saw him."

"That guy sure is full of surprises," Steve says.

"He certainly is."

As I stare at him, I notice his eyes well up.

"No, don't you do that. We promised each other we wouldn't cry."

"I know we did, but it's just, this has been the most amazing month of my life. And I know it's still going to be a couple of months before the show goes to air and we see the final cut, but sharing the screen with you, and living with you in the same house, has been a dream come true for me."

My breath catches in my throat at how sincere Steve is with his words. The look in his eyes is pure love.

"You're so perfect, Steve. Don't let anyone ever tell you otherwise. No matter what happens and how this all plays out, always know that you're very special to me."

I brush my thumb across his cheek, and Steve places his hand on top of mine as he cocks his head to the side.

"Are you going to say that to all the hot, single men you get to flirt with over the next few months?"

"I'm glad you said 'flirt' and not—"

"Watch your mouth, Deacon, we're in an airport. Lots of people around, especially young children."

Leaning in, I kiss his earlobe and snake my arm around his waist, before finally finding those lips that I've enjoyed having wrapped around my cock these past few weeks.

"God, you're making it so—"

"Hard? Wet?" I suggest, in his ear.

"Difficult. You're making it so difficult to say goodbye."

I pull away and look into his beautiful eyes, as I say, "This isn't goodbye, Steve, not by a long shot. Let's think of it as see you soon."

"See you soon? And how soon will that be exactly? A year from now?"

"I don't know. But I promise, when all this is over, and I've got my prize money, I'll come and visit you, every couple of months."

He chuckles and gives me a sheepish grin.

"By the way, just *how much* money do you get after all this is over? Are you allowed to tell me that?"

"I'm not sure, but since you're asking, twelve million."

"Twelve million dollars? Holy fucking shit."

"Yeah. So I'm going to have more than enough money to come and visit you frequently, so don't you dare say your goodbyes."

We sit there for some time, reminiscing about the past month and how much we mean to each other, and our conversation is only interrupted when an announcement over the public address system prompts travelers to Melbourne to head to the gate and prepare to board their plane.

"This is it," Steve says, turning to face me once more.

"Yup."

We stand, and he grabs his bag from beneath the seat.

"I'm going to miss you, Deacon Brady."

"And I'll miss you, Steve Beckett."

I grab hold of his hand and intertwine our fingers as I lean forward and press my lips to his. Every bit of emotion in my body comes to the surface as a tear escapes my eye. I pull away and look at Steve one last time.

"Have a safe flight, and message me when you land."

"I will. And you do the same when you land, wherever it is you're going. And make sure you send lots of photos."

"You bet I will. Goodbye, Steve."

"Goodbye, Deacon," he whispers, he swings his bag over his shoulder.

With a final smile, I wave to Steve as he turns and disappears through the crowd.

As I sit back down on my seat and rest my head against the wall, I feel my phone buzz in my pocket. I pull it out and see Dante's name on the screen.

"Dante?"

"Where are you, Deacon?"

"I just said goodbye to Steve, I'm at the International departures."

"Okay. Can you make your way back to the international terminal, we need to get you checked in and through security."

"Sure. Where are—?" But my words are cut short as he hangs up the phone.

With one final look out the window at the Qantas Boeing 747 that Steve has just boarded, I smile and turn, making my way out of the terminal and off to find Dante.

When I arrive at the international terminal, I find Dante waiting for me by the entrance door.

"Okay, are you ready for your next bachelor?" he asks.

"As ready as I'll ever be. Where exactly are we going?"

He reaches into his coat pocket, pulls out a white envelope and hands it to me. I turn it over and slide out the white card inside. Flipping the card over, I read the message printed on the back.

Deacon Brady,

Are you ready to meet your next bachelor?

Sit back, buckle up, and relax as you head to your next destination…

Paris, France.

ACKNOWLEDGEMENTS

I don't have the flexibility to be able to stay at home and write full time. I wish my life could accommodate that, but when I do get the opportunity to put words into a story, I only hope they're magical. Writing this story came with the help of so many inspirational and talented people.

Sam: Thank you for listening to my constant storytelling updates and being the best friend a guy could ask for.

My work colleagues: Thank you all for being such a spirited, and fun bunch of people to work with. Thank you for your support, advice, and for allowing me to bounce my ideas off you. Most of all, thank you for wanting to read my stories.

Bec: Thank you for taking another chance with my work, and our countless banter. Thank you so much for your good eye and your efficient responses and quick turnaround so that I could publish this book.

Lisa: Thank you for all the final eyes you put into this project, and cleaning up my mess. Thank you for your prompt service and as always, wonderful advice with my writing.

Aria: Thank you for all the final words you put into this project and for being the eyes I could never see.

Ria: You continue to be my biggest supporter, and the backbone to my writing career. Wherever we go, wherever we are, we're there together in the fictional world. You're my rock and roll in book world, as well as my travel companion here and afar whenever we have the opportunity to travel. As always, you help me through everything. You know that none of this would have been possible if I hadn't met you. Thank you for being a kind, loyal and dedicated friend.

Lee: You are without a doubt the most genuine, loyal, and caring colleague I could ever ask for. Thank you for reading my words and encouraging me to continue writing. Thank you for always making me smile. Your friendship, loyalty and dedication will be something I cherish forever.

Danni & Lauren: My beautiful work wives. Thank you both so much for the endless love, support, laughter and of course, friendship. When times are tough, you both make me laugh and shine, even when times are grim.

The readers: Without you, there simply wouldn't be any words. My words are never enough to express how much I appreciate every single one of you, from your shares, reviews, to your messages of support. For those of you that I have had the opportunity to meet in person, whether it be in a book store or at a signing event, THANK YOU for all the love xoxo.

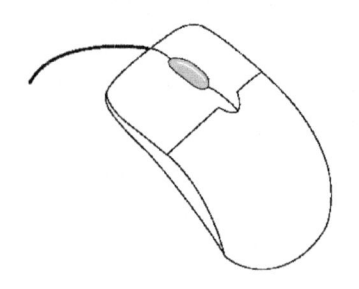

STAY CONNECTED

Here's where you can find J.O Mantel online.

GOODREADS
https://bit.ly/2KtYIw4

AMAZON
https://goo.gl/1nAfPz

TWITTER
http://www.twitter.com/authorjomantel

INSTAGRAM
http://www.instagram.com/authorjomantel

EMAIL
authorjomantel@gmail.com

FACEBOOK
http://www.facebook.com/JO-Mantel-Author

About J.O Mantel

J.O Mantel was born and raised in Melbourne, Australia. As a child, J.O loved reading, and his favorite authors include Roald Dahl, Robin Klein, and Morris Gleitzman. He began writing in 2016 and released his first novel, *First Crush* in the *Dark Falkon Series* that same year. When he is not writing fictional stories, J.O works full time and lives a quiet life on a rural property in Melbourne's northern suburbs.

More by J.O Mantel

THE DARK FALKON SERIES:

First Crush (#1)
Second Best (#2)
Third Act (#3)
Dark Falkon: The Boxed Set (#3.5)

TSUNAMI

ASH

THE FLAMMABLE HEARTS SERIES:

Unexpected Love (#1)

Printed in Great Britain
by Amazon